GOLDEN HART GUIDES
DEVON

GOLDEN HART GUIDES

Devon

SIDGWICK & JACKSON LONDON
in association with Trusthouse Forte

Text by Andrew Franklin, Ronald Pearsall
and Paul Watkins

The publishers gratefully acknowledge
the co-operation of Mr G.J.Paley
and the Devon Tourism Office
for their assistance and advice

Front cover photo: Widecombe-in-the-Moor
Back cover photo: Exmoor, near Lynmouth
Frontispiece: Exeter Cathedral

Photographs by the British Tourist
Authority, with the exception of
ps 10, 12, 15 (Mansell Collection)
51 (lower), 57, 78-79, 82 (Paul Watkins)

Compiled and designed by Paul Watkins
Editorial assistant: Andrew Franklin

First published in Great Britain 1983
by Sidgwick & Jackson in association
with Trusthouse Forte

ISBN 0-283-98911-4

Photoset by Robcroft Ltd, London WC1
Printed and bound in Great Britain
by Hazell Watson and Viney Limited,
Aylesbury, Bucks
for Sidgwick & Jackson Limited,
1 Tavistock Chambers, Bloomsbury Way,
London WC1A 2SG

Contents

Introduction

Devon is the third largest county in England and in its 1,658,000 acres has enormous variety. It is so large and the centre so different from the two coastlines that Devon has something to offer every visitor, and people who come back year after year always find new places to visit and new things to enjoy.

Of all the English counties, Devon is unique in having two separate coastlines. The north coast is the more rugged with spectacular cliff scenery and splendid cliff-top walking. In only a few places do the cliffs open out to form sandy bays, but there – notably at Woolacombe – are some of the finest beaches in the country.

The south coast is much longer than the north (112 miles to 60 miles) and more varied. The best known area is Torbay – the English Riviera – famous for its exceptionally mild climate (which makes it popular all year round), sandy beaches, numerous family activities and luxury hotels. The Imperial in Torquay is England's westernmost 5-star hotel. Although Torquay (and its neighbour Paignton) are the best known of the south Devon resorts, second in popularity in Britain only to Blackpool, there are other coastal centres, each with its own charms and character. Seaton has the River Axe and views of cliffs, Budleigh Salterton and Sidmouth the genteel atmosphere of Edwardian spas, Exmouth and Dawlish are larger and livelier.

On the rivers that run into the sea on the south coast (the Dart, the Teign and the Exe) are fascinating old towns like Topsham, Totnes, Dartmouth and Salcombe, all dating back many centuries and rich in maritime history and architectural interest. But of all Devon's towns, Plymouth and Exeter must rank first. Exeter is a marvellous city, with a medieval cathedral and a university, numerous old churches and fine buildings. Plymouth is bigger – the largest city in the south-west – and today, as in Sir Francis Drake's time, one of the country's major ports for both the Royal Navy and merchant marine.

Dartmoor fills the centre of Devon. Completely different in atmosphere from either coast, the high moor is wild, remote and empty. Only two roads cross it, and the walker who loses himself in the rolling mists can be in serious trouble. Famous for the moorland ponies and sheep, the scenery has a dignity and grandeur which cannot fail to impress the visitor on foot or in a car. On a clear day the views from the highest tors stretch for miles towards both coasts and westwards towards Cornwall. On

Saunton Sands

the edges of Dartmoor are lush green valleys with lively streams (torrential in winter) which have their sources on the moor. On these streams are found some of England's most beautiful and dreamlike villages, with romantic names like Lustleigh, Buckland Monachorum and South Zeal.

Devon has the rare good fortune to have not one but two National Parks within its boundaries. In addition to Dartmoor at the centre, Exmoor lies to the north-east, on the border with Somerset. Less rugged and lower than Dartmoor, Exmoor has a gentler nature, characterised by its green, heathered uplands. Much of the rest of inland Devon, a rural panorama of meadowland, hedged lanes and hidden villages, would itself qualify as a National Park.

Though the scenery, on the coast and inland, is Devon's greatest asset, there is much more besides. The county has a rich architectural heritage, from the small medieval parish churches with their wood-carvings and wooden roofs to the great country houses like Castle Drogo, Powderham Castle and Saltram. In

addition there are a number of attractive and interesting towns, including the old Stannary towns of Ashburton, Lydford, Tavistock and Chagford, and splendid market towns such as South Molton, Great Torrington and Barnstaple. There are fascinating local museums and exhibitions to cater for almost every specialist interest, from aircraft to mechanical music, and a variety of beautiful parks and gardens. There are reminders of Devon's industrial past (which once included tin mining on the southern edge of Dartmoor) at places like Morwellham and Sticklepath, as well as insights into contemporary crafts at the Axminster Carpet Factory and Dartington Glass in Great Torrington.

Details of Devon's many attractions and activities will be found in 'The Best of the Region' section of this book, together with a selection of walks and motoring tours. The Gazetteer provides a round-up of the principal places of interest in the county, and special coverage, with walking tours, is given to Exeter and Plymouth.

Devon

A Brief History

Prehistory The county of Devon has been occupied for at least 100,000 years. At Kent's Cavern in Torquay, fossil remains have been found which date back to the Paleolithic period (Old Stone Age). In addition to human remains, the bones of hyenas, woolly mammoths and bison were found, which shows that the people who lived in the cave (and in similar dwellings in Brixham and near Plymouth) survived by hunting. The advancing glaciers of the Ice Age drove these earliest settlers and the large mammals away from the region, south over the land that then connected Britain to the continent.

From 5000BC New Stone Age (Neolithic) tribesmen inhabited Devon, chiefly in the upland areas of Dartmoor and Exmoor. But like Paleolithic man, they have left few traces of their existence other than long barrows and four chamber tombs, of which Spinster's Rock is the most impressive. These chamber tombs (there are many more good examples in Cornwall) consist of four or five vast upright stone blocks with a horizontal capstone on top. They were used for mass-burial.

In the Bronze Age, Dartmoor was also extensively occupied, and from this period date most of the many prehistoric sites on the high moor. Grimspound, the best known, was an enclosure of a number of hut circles. Most of the huts would have been lived in, but some were used for storage and animals. Archeologists cannot agree whether the outer wall around this and similar camps was for defence or simply to enclose livestock.

Exeter Cathedral

The first Celts arrived in the county from Ireland and Brittany from about 450 BC. They brought the Iron Age with their new iron tools and weapons. Their major site was Hembury Fort, which they strongly fortified with ramparts and an elaborate entrance. But they also had a town, nothing more than a hamlet by today's standards, but the only one in the south-west. When the Romans colonised it they called it Isca Dumnoniorum, after the name they gave to the Celtic tribes. Today it is called Exeter.

The Romans Although Julius Caesar landed a raiding party in Kent in 54 BC, the Romans did not conquer Britain until 43 AD, under Emperor Claudius. But within a decade of occupation a Roman garrison had been established at Isca Dumnoniorum. During the next 200 years it grew to be a fully-fledged Roman town with a central carfax or crossroads and city walls (which still partially stand today). Exeter was the westernmost outpost of civilisation. Although trade was conducted with the Celtic tin-miners of Cornwall and minor roads were built through north Devon, there were no towns or settlements and only four villas have been found west of the city. When the Romans left England after 410 AD to defend their beleaguered imperial city, they left good roads connecting Exeter to Salisbury and London (today's A30, or parts of it) and a new faith: Christianity.

Although the Angles, Saxons and other European invaders of the south-east were pagans, the Celts remained loyal to Christianity, and were therefore receptive to the 'Coming of the Saints' from Wales, Brittany and Ireland. Most of the religious activity (miracles and martyrdoms) was centred on Cornwall, but some of it spilled over into western Devon. Thus churches are dedicated to St Nectan at Hartland and Ashcombe, to St Winifred at Branscombe, to St Brannock at Braunton and to St Petrock at Parracombe. The Celts did not build churches: the saints lived in crude dwellings, sworn to chastity and poverty, and their religious devotions were often centred on carved crosses. Sadly, while many fine Celtic crosses remain in Cornwall, there are no good ones left in Devon.

The Anglo-Saxons and Danes In the early 7th century the Saxons began their colonisation of Devon, arriving by boat in the southern river estuaries and overland by the old Roman roads. In 658, after Celtic resistance, they captured Exeter, renaming it Escanceaster. Unlike the Celts, the Saxons were great church builders, although nothing remains above foundation level of any of their work in the county. Most important and grandest of their churches was Crediton Minster, which was consecrated in 739 and made the centre of a vast see covering all of Devon and Cornwall in 909.

But the Saxons, who conquered the country by military might, were themselves threatened by the military superiority of the Danes. Throughout the 9th century Danish invaders raided Devon from the sea, and in 876 sacked Exeter before being beaten back by Alfred the Great. There is evidence to suggest that the Danes were aided by the native Celts, who were oppressed by the Saxons and wanted to be rid of them. But worse was to come. In 997 the Danes destroyed Tavistock Abbey, and six years later ravaged Exeter again with ferocious thoroughness. Ultimately King Canute conquered the whole country and it was not until his death (1035) and the re-establishment of an independent Anglo-Saxon kingdom that the region recovered. The rebuilt town of Exeter, with its superior defensive site, became, in 1050, the new bishopric in place of Crediton.

William the Conqueror After his victory at Hastings in 1066, William did not find a compliant state at his feet. Devon refused to recognise the new king and despite its past record remained loyal to the Saxon cause. In 1068 William marched on Devon and besieged Exeter. The city was heroically defended by Gytha, the mother of King Harold, but eventually had to surrender. To prevent any further trouble and to provide a safe home for the Norman nobility, William built castles in Totnes, Okehampton and Barnstaple and Rougemont Castle in Exeter.

Norman religious houses were also established. There were 35 monasteries and three nunneries, remains of many of which can be seen throughout the county. (A typical example is Hartland Abbey, which once owned much of north-west Devon but is now a ruin incorporated in a private house.)

Shipwreck on the Plymouth Sound

The Middle Ages: wool and tin
This period of growth saw the foundation of many of Devon's towns and major churches. Earlier, the Domesday Book Survey of the county (1086) had recorded only one town: Exeter, with a mere 26 dwellings. But over the next 300 years Okehampton, Barnstaple and Totnes grew into sizeable market towns (each around its castle), as did towns like Moretonhampstead, Bideford, Kingsbridge and Torrington. All were at the centre of rich agricultural areas, for at this time Devon's prosperity rested on sheep, which were grazed all over the county. Throughout the Middle Ages England supplied wool and cloth to all Europe, and Devon wool was at the forefront. Sheep continued to predominate right up to the 19th century when the competition from Australian wool, and the lack of coal in the county for textile mills to compete with those in the north of England, made sheep-rearing uneconomic. Farmers then switched to cows, and beef and dairy cattle are now found where sheep once grazed.

The other great medieval industry was tin-mining, although the industry did not have the same importance as in neighbouring Cornwall. In the Middle Ages the miners or 'tinners' were exempt from normal taxes but had to pay special stamp duty on their ore twice a year at one of the four Stannary towns (Ashburton, Lydford, Tavistock and Chagford). Apart from this external control, the tinners managed their own affairs and had a 'Stannary Parliament' and 'Court' which met regularly at Lydford. Wrongdoers were imprisoned in Lydford Castle, a grim tower built expressly for the purpose and from which few prisoners came out alive. Dartmoor was the centre of the tin-mining, and the ruined 19th-century engine houses are romantic reminders of the industry. For a while there was also a copper boom centred around Morwellham Quay on the Tamar, and a canal was built across Dartmoor to Tavistock to carry the ore. But the boom was short-lived and petered out soon after it had begun. Silver was mined for some years at Combe Martin on the north coast, but by the beginning of this century the extraction of precious metals had ceased to be economic in the face of much more accessible ores in Africa (silver and copper) and Malaysia (tin). Today only china clay and granite are quarried, the former leaving vast unsightly tips to the north of Plymouth.

Elizabethan seafaring Elizabeth I's reign was without doubt the golden age of Devon. The Reformation had afforded great opportunities for the gentry when the abbeys and monasteries were dissolved and their lands and properties sold by an impoverished crown. Thus Tavistock Abbey and its lands were acquired by the Russell family, later to become the Dukes of Bedford (their more famous seat Woburn Abbey was also a former religious property), and Sir Francis Drake acquired Buckland Abbey.

Primarily, the wealth and fame of Devon's great men came not from the land but the sea. This was the era of Sir Francis Drake (born in Tavistock), Sir Richard Grenville (Bideford), Hawkins and Frobisher. They were all great sea-captains and privateers, patrolling the south coast and the Atlantic and attacking foreign shipping for the rich pickings of treasure from the New World. In addition there were the heroic exploratory expeditions, such as Drake's circumnavigation of the globe and William Burroughs' discovery of the Arctic coast of Russia.

In 1588 the Spanish assembled one of the biggest fleets in history – the Armada – to invade England. It was in Plymouth Sound (Sutton Harbour) that Drake kept the English fleet waiting while he played bowls as the Armada sailed past. (It is worth noting that this was not an act of bravado but the calculated move of a brilliant tactician. The superb natural harbour at Plymouth hid the English fleet from the Spanish, and once they had sailed past, the English fleet was able to bombard the Armada from behind while the following wind prevented the Spanish ships from counter-attacking). The defeat of the Armada heralded the growth of Plymouth. From then on it became a major naval port and to this day has been one of the most important bases of the Royal Navy.

Non-Industrial Revolutions The county remained important in the 17th century. With Devon's strong Puritan tradition, it was appropriate that the Pilgrim Fathers should sail from Plymouth in 1620 (after an abortive first attempt from Dartmouth) and in the Civil War Devon was evenly divided between Parliament and the King. Plymouth and Exeter supported Cromwell, but much of the gentry and nobility backed the monarch.

In the country the poorer people tended to follow their squire or landlord. The Civil War split many families, and it was a long time before the divisions healed. The next revolution, the 'Glorious' or 'Bloodless Revolution' of 1688 when James II was deposed by William of Orange, began in Devon when the Dutch king landed in Brixham.

In the 18th and 19th centuries, when the Industrial Revolution was converting the north and Midlands into the manufacturing centre of the Empire and the world, there was little or no development in Devon. The roads were hardly better than they had been in Roman times, and there was no route (except unmarked shepherds' and tinners' tracks) across Dartmoor until French prisoners in chain gangs built one in the 1780s. The advent of Brunel's railway in the mid-19th century had little effect on the development of industry. Without coal, Devon had no means of firing the foundries and mills necessary for manufacture. The county remained a rural backwater.

In the 18th century Devon's isolation did, however, foster one industry: smuggling. Both of Devon's coasts were extensively used by 'fair-traders' landing tobacco, diamonds, lace, and most of all, brandy and spirits. Often whole villages were involved, and there was normally little support for the excise officers or 'preventive men', who consequently had to rely on informers. One of the most notorious areas for smuggling was Beer: the master smuggler there made so much money that he was able to retire and write his memoirs.

Tourism The better organisation of the customs men brought the decline of smuggling in the 19th century. But in its place grew a new and much more important industry – tourism.

The first travellers went to spas like Buxton, Harrogate and Bath, ostensibly to 'take the waters'. But in the late 18th century the fashion changed and sea-bathing became popular as a cure for all sorts of ailments. In 1763 Tobias Smollett proudly wrote that 'I hired a chaise, and going to the beach, about a league from the town, plunged into the sea without hesitation. By this desperate remedy I got a fresh cold in my head but my stitches and fever vanished.'

Exmouth was the first resort to develop, and benefited from the boost it received when Lady Byron and Lady Nelson, both fashionable society ladies, moved there early in the 19th century. An assembly room opened shortly afterwards. Teignmouth, patronised by Keats and Fanny Burney, followed next and also opened assembly rooms. Sidmouth did better still with its royal visitors: King George III and Princess (later Queen) Victoria. Torquay, the biggest of all the resorts, is said to have been built up by the families of officers of the British fleet stationed in Torbay awaiting Napoleon's threatened invasion.

The Napoleonic Wars generally had a good effect on the resorts: with the continent closed to travellers the West Country became a popular alternative destination. The north coast also opened up, but not until Victorian times, with Ilfracombe as the main holiday centre. All along the coast, boarding houses and hotels were built, winter gardens opened and day excursions organised, first by carriage, then by charabanc. But it was not until the advent of universal paid holidays, good roads and widespread car ownership that Devon became accessible to all.

19th-century Torquay

15

The Best of the Region

excluding Cities of Exeter (p. 56) and Plymouth (p. 78)

A summary of the places of interest in the region, open to the public. The location, with map reference, and description of each place, is shown in the Gazetteer. Names in bold are Gazetteer entries, and those with an asterisk are considered to be of outstanding interest. (NT) indicates properties owned by the National Trust

W front, Exeter Cathedral

Churches

Those listed here are specially worth a visit, either for the building itself, or for a particular feature such as brasses, heraldry, tombs or wall-paintings

Ashburton St Andrew

Ashcombe St Nectan

Berry Pomeroy St Mary

Bovey Tracey St Thomas

Branscombe St Winifred

Braunton St Brennock

Buckfast Abbey

Chagford St Michael

Clovelly All Saints

Combe Martin St Peter ad Vincula

Crediton Holy Cross

Cullompton St Andrew

Dartmouth St Saviour

Doddiscombsleigh St Michael

Exeter see p.56

Great Torrington St Michael

Hartland St Nectan

Lewtrenchard St Peter

Molland St Mary

Mortehoe St Mary Magdalene

Ottery St Mary St Mary

Parracombe St Petrock

Plymouth see p.78

Swimbridge St James

Tavistock St Eustace

Tawstock St Peter

Tiverton St Peter

Totnes St Mary

Trentishoe St Peter

Widecombe-in-the-Moor St Pancras

Historic Houses

Admission to most historic houses is between £1-2 (Children half-price).

Arlington Court (NT)
Apr-Oct, Sun-Fri 11-6

Bicton
See *Parks, Gardens & Wildlife*

Bickleigh Bickleigh Castle
Easter-May, Wed, Sun & Bank Hol Mon; Jun-early Oct, Sun-Fri 2-5

*Buckland Abbey (NT)
Easter-Sep, Mon-Sat 11-6, Sun 2-6; Oct-Easter, Wed, Sat, Sun 2-5

Cadhay House
Mid Jul-Aug, Wed & Thur; Spring & Summer Bank Hol Sun & Mon 2-6

*Castle Drogo (NT)
Apr-Oct, daily 11-6

Chambercombe Manor
Easter-Sep, Mon-Fri 10.30-5, Sun 2-5

Cockington Cockington Court
Café daily 10-5; grounds dawn-dusk

Compton Castle (NT)
Apr-Oct, Mon, Wed, Thur 10-12 & 2-5

Dartington Hall
All year 9-dusk except when in use

Ermington Flete
May-Sep, Wed & Thur 2-5

Exeter see p.56

Exmouth A La Ronde
Easter-Oct, Mon-Sat 10-6 & Sun 2-7

Killerton House (NT)
House Apr-Oct, daily 11-6; grounds daily during daylight

Knightshayes Court (NT)
Apr-Oct, daily: house 1.30-6; garden 11-6

Newton Abbot Bradley Manor (NT)
Apr-Sep, Wed 2-5

Paignton Kirkham House
Apr-Sep, Mon-Sat 9.30-6.30 & Sun 2-6.30

Paignton Oldway Mansion
Mon-Sat 9-1 & 2.15-5.15 & May-Sep, Sun 2.30-5

Plymouth see p.78

Powderham Castle
Easter Sun & Mon, Sun only until mid May, then Sun-Thur until late Sep, 2-6

*Saltram House (NT)
Apr-Oct: house Bank Hol Mon, Tue-Sun 12.30-6; garden daily 11-6

Tapeley Park
Easter-Oct, Tue-Sun & Bank Hols 10-6

Tiverton Castle
Easter weekend, mid May-Sep, Sun-Thur 2.30-5.30

Torquay Torre Abbey
Apr-Oct, 10-1 & 2-5.30

*Ugbrooke House
May Bank Hol Sun & Mon, Jun-Sep, Sun-Thur: house 2-5.30; grounds 12-5.30

Parks, Gardens & Wildlife

Admission to the gardens of historic houses is usually included in a combined ticket for house and garden. (See admission to historic houses above.) Where the garden can be visited separately this is usually about half the price of the combined ticket. The entrance fee for other gardens open to the public is usually in the range 30-50p (Children half-price or less).

Arlington Court (NT)
House & garden. See *Historic Houses*

*Bicton Gardens
Apr-Oct, daily 10-6

Bovey Tracey Yarner Wood
Nature Reserve
All times

Brixham Aquarium & Trawling Exhibition
Easter & summer, daily 10-10

*Clovelly Hobby Drive
Easter-Oct, Mon-Fri 9-5

Cockington Cockington Court
House & garden. *See Historic Houses*

Combe Martin Buzzacott Manor
Woolly Monkey Park
Easter-Sep, daily 10-5

Combe Martin Higher Leigh Manor
Woolly Monkey Sanctuary
Easter-Oct, daily 10-5.30

*Dartington Hall
House & garden. *See Historic Houses*

Dartmoor Wildlife Park Sparkwell
Daily 10-dusk

Dunsford Dunsford Wood Nature
Reserve
All times

Eggesford Eggesford Forest Nature
Trail
All times

Exmoor Bird Gardens
Daily 10-dusk

Farway Countryside Park
Easter-Sep, Sun-Fri 10-6

Gnome Reserve West Putford
Easter-Sep, Sun-Fri 10-1 & 2-6, also
Jul-Aug 7pm-9pm

Ilfracombe Bicclescombe Park
Tropical Wildlife Garden
Easter-Sep, daily 10-dusk

*Killerton House (NT)
House and garden. See *Historic Houses*

Knightshayes Court (NT)
House & garden. See *Historic Houses*

Marwood Hill Gardens
Mar-Oct, 9-dusk

Paignton Aquarium
Easter, May-Sep, daily 10-10

Paignton Zoo
Winter, daily 10-5; Summer, daily 10-7.30

Parracombe Cowley Cleave Nature
Trail
All times

Powderham Castle
House & garden. See *Historic Houses*

River Dart Country Park
Apr-Sep, daily 10-6

Rosemoor Gardens
Apr-Oct, daily 10-dusk

Salcombe Overbecks Garden (NT)
See *Museums & Galleries*

Saltram House (NT)
House & garden. See *Historic Houses*

Shaldon Wildlife Collection
Easter-Sep, daily 10-6; Oct-Easter,
daily 11-4

Sidmouth Donkey Sanctuary
Daily 9-5

*Slapton Ley Nature Reserve
All times

Staverton Riverford Farm
All Bank Hols, mid Apr-Jun, Mon,
Tue & Thur; Jul-Aug, daily; tours
begin 2.30

Tapeley Park
See *Historic Houses*

Teignmouth Aquarium
Easter, May-Sep daily 10.30-6.30

Torquay Aqualand
Apr-Sep, daily 10-7, Oct-Mar

Ugbrooke House
House & garden. See *Historic Houses*

Yealmpton Devon Shire Horse Farm
Centre
See *Industrial & Rural Heritage*

Castles, Ruins & Ancient Sites

Unless otherwise stated, these sites are
accessible at all reasonable times.

Berry Pomeroy Castle
Medieval castle ruins
Daily Mar-Oct 9-6; Nov-Feb 9.30-4

Bickleigh Bickleigh Castle
See *Historic Houses*

Blackbury Castle
Iron Age fort

Clovelly Clovelly Dykes
Iron Age settlement

Compton Castle (NT)
See *Historic Houses*

Countisbury Countisbury Camp
Prehistoric fort

*Dartmouth Dartmouth Castle
Mid Mar-mid Oct, Mon-Sat 9.30-
6.30, Sun 2-6.30; mid Oct-mid Mar,
Mon-Sat 9.30-4, Sun 2-4

Drewsteignton Fingle Bridge
Clapper bridge .

Exeter see p. 56

Hallsands
Deserted coastal village

Hembury Fort
Prehistoric hill fort

Lydford Lydford Castle

*Okehampton Okehampton Castle
Norman castle ruins
Times as for Dartmouth Castle

Plymouth see p.78

Plympton Castle
Norman castle ruins

*Postbridge Clapper bridge, and 2m S
at Bellever

Salcombe Salcombe Castle

*Spinster's Rock
Prehistoric burial site

Tiverton Tiverton Castle
See *Historic Houses*

Torquay Kent's Cavern
Easter-Jun, daily 10-6; Jun-Sep 10-9
(Sat 6); Sep-Easter 10-5

*Totnes Totnes Castle
Times as for Dartmouth Castle

Woodbury Woodbury Castle
Iron Age fort

Yealmpton Kitley Caves
Easter week & Sat before Spring
Bank Hol-Sep, 10-5.30

Museums & Galleries

Appledore North Devon Maritime
Museum
Easter-Sep, daily 2.30-5.30, also Tue-
Fri 11-1

Ashburton Museum
Mid May-Sep, Tue, Thur, Fri & Sat
2.30-5

Barnstaple North Devon Athenaeum
Mon-Sat 10-1 & Mon, Wed-Fri 2.15-5

Barnstaple St Anne's Museum
Spring Bank Hol-Sep, Mon-Sat 10-1 &
2-4.30

Bicton Gardens Country Life and
Transport Museum
See *Parks, Gardens & Wildlife*

Bideford Burton Art Gallery
Mon-Fri 10-1 & 2-5, Sat 10-12.45

Braunton Braunton & District
Museum
Easter, May-Sep, Mon-Fri 10-5

Brixham Aquarium & Trawling
Exhibition
See *Parks, Gardens & Wildlife*

Brixham Museum
Easter-mid-Oct, daily 10-5.30

Buckfast Abbey Museum of Shellcraft
Easter-Oct, daily 10-6

Budleigh Salterton Fairlynch Museum
Easter-Oct, daily 2.30-5, also Jul-Aug
10.30-12.30

Croyde Gem, Rock and Shell Museum
Mar-Oct, daily 10-5

Dartmouth Museum
May-Oct, Mon-Sat 11-5; Nov-Apr,
Mon-Sat 2.15-4

Dartmouth Henley Museum
Mon-Sat 2-4

Dawlish Museum
May-Sep, Mon-Sat 10-12.30 & 2-5,
Sun 2-5

Dawlish South Devon Railway
Museum
See *Transport Heritage*

Exeter see p.56

Exmouth Sandy Bay Steam and
Country Life Museum
See *Industrial & Rural Heritage*

Great Torrington Museum
May-Sep, Mon-Fri 10-12.45 & 2.15-
4.45, Sat 10-12.45

Hartland Hartland Quay Museum
Easter, Spring Bank Hol-Sep, daily

Holsworthy Devon Museum of
Mechanical Music
Easter-Sep, 10.30-12.30 & 2-5

Honiton All Hallows Museum
Easter weekend, mid May-Sep, Mon-
Sat 10-5

Ilfracombe Museum
Easter-Oct, daily 10-5; Nov-Easter,
daily 10-1

*Kingsbridge Cookworthy Museum
Easter-Oct, Mon-Sat 10-5

Lynmouth and Lynton Lyn and
Exmoor Museum
Apr-Sep, Mon-Fri 10-12.30 & 2-5,
Sun 2-5

Morwellham Quay
See *Industrial & Rural Heritage*

Okehampton Museum of Dartmoor Life
May-Oct, Mon-Sat 10.30-4.30

Plymouth see p.78

Salcombe Overbecks (NT)
Apr-Oct, daily 11-1 & 2-6

Shebbear Alscott Farm Museum
See *Industrial & Rural Heritage*

Sidmouth Museum
Easter-Sep, Mon-Sat 10.30-12.30 & 2.30-4.30, Sun 2.30-4.30

South Molton Guildhall Museum
Mon-Sat 11-12.30 & 2.30-4.30

Sticklepath Finch Foundry Trust and Museum of Rural History
See *Industrial & Rural Heritage*

Teignmouth Museum
Apr-Oct, Tue-Fri 10-12.30 & 2.30-5

*****Tiverton** Museum
Mon-Sat (not Bank Hol) 10.30-4.30

Topsham Museum
Tue, Wed & Sat 2-5

Torbay Aircraft Museum
Easter-Sep, daily 10-6; Oct-Easter 10-4

Torquay Museum
Mon-Fri 10-5, also May-Oct Sat 10-5

Totnes Devonshire Collection of Period Costume
May-Sep, Mon-Sat 11-5

*****Totnes** Elizabethan House Museum
Mar-Oct, daily 10.30-1 & 2-5.30

Totnes Motor Museum
Easter-Oct, daily 10-5

Yelverton Paperweight Centre
Easter-Oct, Mon-Sat 10-5

Industrial & Rural Heritage

Axminster Carpet Factory
Tours Mon-Fri 9.30-12 & 2-5

Bickleigh Bickleigh Mill Craft Centre and Farm
Jan-Mar, daily 2-5; Apr-Dec 10-6

Budleigh Salterton Otterton Mill
Summer, daily 11-5.30; winter 2-5.30

Chudleigh 'The Wheel' Mill and Craft Centre
Apr-Oct, daily 10-6; Nov-Mar 10-5

Dartington Hall Tweed Mill
Tours Mon-Fri 9-12.30 & 1.30-5

Dartmouth Newcomen Engine House
Easter-Oct, Mon-Sat 11-5, Sun 2-5

Eggesford Ashley Countryside Collection
Easter-Oct, Mon, Wed, Sat & Sun 10-6

Exmouth Sandy Bay Steam and Countryside Museum
Easter, Spring Bank Hol-Sep, daily 10.30-5

Grand Western Canal
See *Transport Heritage*

*****Great Torrington** Dartington Glass
Tours Mon-Fri 9.30-10.30 & 12-3.30

Hele Watermill
Easter-Sep, Mon-Fri 10-5, Sun 2-5

Ilfracombe Bicclescombe Park Watermill
Spring Bank Hol-Sep, daily 10.30-1 & 2.15-5.15

Lynmouth Ancient Smithy
May-mid Sep, Sun-Fri 10-5

Mary Tavy Wheal Betsy Engine House
Daily all times

*****Morwellham Quay**
Summer, daily 10-6; winter 10-4

Postbridge Relics of Vitifer Tin Mines
Daily all times

Seaton Seaton & District Electric Tramway
See *Transport Heritage*

Shebbear Alscott Farm Museum
Easter-Sep, daily 12-dusk

*****Sticklepath** Finch Foundry Trust and Museum of Rural Industry
Daily 11-5.30

Uffculme Coldharbour Mill
Easter-Oct, daily 11-5; Oct-Easter, Wed-Sun 11-5

Yealmpton Devon Shire Horse Farm Centre
Mid Mar-Nov, daily 10-5

Transport Heritage

Beer Beer Heights Light Railway
May Bank Hol-Oct, Mon-Fri 10-5.30

Buckfastleigh Riverside Miniature
Railway
Easter, May-Oct, daily 11.30-5

Bicton Gardens Country Life and
Transport Museum
See *Parks, Gardens & Wildlife*

*Dart Valley Railway
Both lines: Easter weekend,
May Bank Hol; Jun & Jul, most days;
Aug, weekends only; Sep, most days.
For timetable – Dart Valley Line,
Tel (03644) 2338; Torbay and
Dartmouth Line, Tel (0803) 555872

Dawlish South Devon Railway
Museum and Model Railway
Easter, Jun-Sep, daily 10-dusk

Exmouth 'The Maer' 00 Model
Railway
Easter-Oct, daily 10.30-dusk

*Grand Western Canal
Park, always open. Horseboat trips
Apr-Sep most days. Timetable: Tel
(0884) 253345

Kingsbridge Miniature Railway
May-Sep, daily 11-5

*Lynmouth and Lynton Cliff Railway
Daily all year

*Seaton Seaton & District Electric
Tramway
Frequent service all year

Natural Features

Many of these famous beauty spots are
only reached by foot, particularly those
on Dartmoor. For details of access
(unrestricted unless otherwise stated)
see Gazetteer.

*Becky Falls Waterfall on Dartmoor

Berry Head Coastal promontory

*Braunton Braunton Burrows, sand
dunes on NW coast

Burgh Island Small island off S coast

Countisbury Foreland Point, headland
on N coast

Clovelly Gallantry Bower, combe

Cranmere Pool Remote pool in peat
bog at heart of Dartmoor

*Dartmoor

*Exmoor

Hartland Speke's Mill Mouth,
waterfall. Hartland Point, headland on
NW coast

*Haytor Dartmoor tor

Heddon's Mouth (NT) Valley on N
coast

Hound Tor Dartmoor tor

Lee Bay N coast bay

*Lundy Island (NT) Island 20m W of
N coast

*Lydford Lydford Gorge (NT)
Apr-Oct, daily 9-5.30

*Lynmouth and Lynton Valley of the
Rocks and Lyn Valley Gorges (NT)

Manaton Bowerman's Nose,
Dartmoor Tor

Saunton Sands on NW coast

Shaldon Smuggler's Tunnel, natural
cliff tunnel

Slapton Ley Freshwater lake by sea

Torquay Kent's Cavern, limestone
caves
See *Castles, Ruins & Ancient Sites*

Wistman's Wood Primeval Dartmoor
oak wood

*Woolacombe Barracane Beach and
Woolacombe Downs, golden sand
beaches and cliffs on NW coast

Yealmpton Kitley Caves
See *Castles, Ruins & Ancient Sites*

Famous Connections

Many famous – or simply unusual – personalities have been connected with Devon throughout its history. Details of their association will be found under the Gazetteer entries.

Austen, Jane Teignmouth

Baring-Gould, Rev S. Lewtrenchard

Byron, Lady Exmouth

Chichester, Sir Francis Arlington Court

Coleridge, Samuel Taylor Ottery St Mary

Dickens, Charles Clovelly and Dawlish

Drake, Sir Francis Buckland Abbey and Plymouth

Galsworthy, John Manaton

Keats, John Dawlish and Teignmouth

Kingsley, Charles Clovelly, Bideford and Westward Ho!

Kipling, Rudyard Westward Ho!

Nelson, Lady Exmouth

Raleigh, Sir Walter Budleigh Salterton

Reynolds, Sir Joshua Plympton and Saltram House

The Royal Family: King George VI, The Duke of Edinburgh, Prince Charles and Prince Andrew Britannia Royal Naval College, Dartmouth

Russell, Rev Jack Swimbridge

Victoria, Queen Sidmouth

Hotels & Historic Inns

(including Exeter and Plymouth)

†Non-residential inn
(THF) A Trusthouse Forte Hotel

Barnstaple
Imperial Hotel (THF)
Taw Vale Parade, Barnstaple
EX32 8NB
Tel (0271) 5861

The long white frontage on the riverside is one of the attractions of this favourite tourist haunt, sometimes referred to as the 'Queen of the West'. The hotel, with 56 rooms, has great individuality and charm. Its comfortable, gracious building is Edwardian with spacious rooms, long windows and wrought iron balconies, but the interior designs and furnishings are entirely modern.

Burgh Island
The Pilchard Inn
Burgh Island, Bigbury-on-Sea
TQ7 4AU
Tel (054881) 344

Built in 1336 as monks' lodgings: after the Dissolution the island and its sole building fell into the hands of smugglers and the pirate Tom Crocker. The skull and cross-bones on the inn sign are a reminder of his activities. There is now a large hotel annexe.

Combe Martin
†*The Pack of Cards*
High Street, Combe Martin EX34 0ET
Tel (027188) 3327

Unusual 17th-c. pub commemorating the local landlord's obsession with gambling. There are four floors (one for each suit), each with 13 doors, and there were originally 52 windows, although some were blocked up to avoid window tax in the 18th-c. Good home-made food.

Dartington
The Cott Inn
Dartington, Totnes TQ9 6HE
Tel (0803) 863777

One of the oldest inns in the country, established in the early 14th-c. Cider was once brewed here for ¼p per gallon. Cock-fighting (on which huge sums of money were wagered) also took place until the last century. It is claimed that Daniel Defoe wrote *Robinson Crusoe* while staying here. Good bar snacks and separate restaurant.

Dartmouth

†*The Cherub*
High Street, Dartmouth TQ6 9RB
Tel (08043) 2571

The oldest building in Dartmouth, formerly a wool merchant's house. Constructed of oak timbers c. 1380, it retains most of the original timbers, exposed inside and out. Specialities include fresh crab.

Dart Marina Hotel (THF)
Sandquay, Dartmouth TQ6 9PH
Tel (08043) 2580

An ideal headquarters for the sailing fraternity, this attractive 37-room hotel stands in a lovely position facing the quay and the slipways to the estuary. All the requirements for pleasure sailing are at hand. There are fine views from the lounge, bar and restaurant towards the hills on the far banks of the Dart.

Exeter

†*The Ship Inn*
Martin's Lane, Exeter EX1 1EY
Tel (0392) 72040

In St Martin's Lane on the edge of the cathedral precincts, the 15th-c. half-timbered *Ship Inn* was a favourite haunt of Drake, Raleigh, Hawkins, Frobisher and other seaman adventurers, who met here in the late 16th-c. to plan raids and expeditions. Good restaurant-bar on the 1st floor.

Exmouth

Imperial Hotel (THF)
The Esplanade, Exmouth EX8 2SW
Tel (03952) 74761

Designed by two sons of Sir Charles Barry (the architect of the Houses of Parliament) the 61-room hotel was opened in 1869 to meet the growing demand for accommodation by holidaymakers and businessmen. It stands in 4 acres of beautiful grounds overlooking Lyme Bay. There are many facilities for children, and a heated open-air swimming pool.

Lynmouth

The Rising Sun
Mars Hill, Lynmouth EX35 6EQ
Tel (05985) 3223

Washed away in the terrible flood of 1952, this 14th-c. building was faithfully reconstructed with a new thatched roof and the original oak panelling in the bars. Formerly a cottage, R.D. Blackmore is said to have written *Lorna Doone* here, and Shelley and his wife Mary Godwin stayed here on their honeymoon. Real ales, and a separate restaurant.

Paignton

Palace Hotel (THF)
Esplanade Road, Paignton TQ4 6BJ
Tel (0803) 555121

Facing a 5m stretch of safe sandy beach, this splendid white building was once the home of the American millionaire Isaac Merritt Singer, founder of the sewing machine industry. It became a hotel in 1952 and its interior still reflects the splendour of its original appointments. Standing in a 2-acre garden, it is an excellent family holiday centre.

Plymouth

Mayflower Post House Hotel (THF)
The Hoe, Plymouth PL1 3DL
Tel (0752) 662828

Rising ten storeys above the Hoe where Drake once played his famous game of bowls, this modern hotel designed for holidaymakers and businessmen alike occupies one of the finest sites in Britain. From many of its 104 rooms, guests can enjoy superb views over Plymouth Sound. The hotel opened in 1970 during the celebrations which marked the 350th anniversary of the Pilgrims Fathers' voyage.

†*The Three Crowns*
11 The Parade, The Barbican
Plymouth PL1 2JL
Tel (0752) 29324

One of a number of ancient sailors' pubs in the old harbour – The Barbican. From here Sir Francis Drake sailed out to defeat the Spanish Armada, and the Pilgrim Fathers left for America. The 18th-c. façade hides the more venerable origins of the pub.

Postbridge
†*The Warren House Inn*
Postbridge, Yelverton PL20 6TN
Tel (0822) 88208

Over 500 years old, the inn once
served the tin miners on the high
moor. Although on the main road, it is
miles from the nearest house and has
been a life-saving refuge for many
walkers lost in mist on the moor. The
peat fire in the inglenook has been
kept burning since 1846. Wholesome
snacks; hikers and children welcome.

South Zeal
The Oxenham Arms
South Zeal, Okehampton EX20 1JT
Tel (083784) 244

Built as a monastery, then a manor
house for the Burgoyne family, the
present building is 16th-17th-c. and
has stone-mullioned windows and a
large portico. It is the most stately
building in the village and appears in
two novels: Charles Kingsley's
Westward Ho! and S. Baring-Gould's
John Herring, both very popular in the
last century. Excellent bar food.

Tavistock
Bedford Hotel (THF)
Plymouth Road, Tavistock PL19 8BB
Tel (0822) 3221

This imposing 32-room stone-built
hotel is steeped in history and stands
on the original site of the famous
Tavistock Abbey. After the
Dissolution, the Dukes of Bedford
acquired the abbey lands and in the
18th-c. the original buildings were
pulled down and the house rebuilt in
its present style. An old stone porch
and the 15th-c. abbey gateway remain.

Torquay
The Imperial (THF)
Park Hill Road, Torquay TQ1 2OG
Tel (0803) 24301

Over the years many royal and famous
personages have stayed in this
exclusive resort hotel that boasts 5-star
comforts, food and service. It is
renowned for its programme of
gastronomic weekends. Standing in
5½ acres of sub-tropical garden, the
hotel opened in 1866 but has since
been thoroughly modernised. It has
panoramic views across Torbay.

Sport & Recreation

Boating The Torridge at Bideford is
ideal for rowing-boats, while the
Rivers Exe, Dart and Tamar all have
stretches where dinghies can be hired.
The county's irregular and sheltered S
coastline offers excellent sailing, and
most of the resorts have sailing clubs.
The principal centres are Shaldon,
Starcross, Exmouth, Dartmouth,
Kingswear, Plymouth and Salcombe.
On the more exposed N coast the best
centres are on the Taw and Torridge
estuaries at Bideford, Appledore and
Instow.

Fishing Trout fishing is available on
many of the rivers of Devon, and some
salmon on those which have their
source in Dartmoor. The many
reservoirs, especially those in and
around Dartmoor, are also well
stocked with fish. Boats can be hired
for sea-fishing at Brixham, Plymouth
and Salcombe, and deep-water anglers
can be taken out to reefs and wrecks.
Shark fishing is available off the S
coast. There is excellent coarse fishing
at Slapton Ley, long renowned for its
pike. For further information on
freshwater fishing contact the South-
West Water Authority, 3-5 Barnfield
Road, Exeter (Tel (0392) 31666).

Golf There are numerous golf clubs in
Devon, most of which welcome non-
members. Most are sited near the
coast, and some, like that at Westward
Ho! have an international reputation.
Budleigh Salterton is famed for both
its golf and croquet facilities.

Riding Hacking, hunting and pony-
trekking are available throughout the
region. Pony-trekking is concentrated
on Dartmoor and Exmoor, with many
stables offering full tuition.

Surfing is best on the NW coast off the
beaches of Woolacombe, Croyde and
Appledore.

Skin-diving The large number of
wrecks around the Devon coast are a
great attraction to skin-divers.
Instruction in the sport is given by
experienced divers in Dartmouth and
Plymouth: information is available
from the local tourist offices.

Festivals and Events

April *Crediton* Great Market (3rd Sat)

May *Budleigh Salterton* Gala Week (Spring Bank Hol week); *Plymouth* Lord Mayor's Day; *Tavistock* Carnival

June *Ashburton* Ale-tasting and Bread-weighing Ceremony (end Jun)

July *Buckland Monachorum* Fair (2nd or 3rd Sat) *Holsworthy* St Peter's Fair; *Honiton* Annual Fair (3rd week); *Kingsbridge* Three Day Fair (3rd week); *Newton Abbot* Carnival Week (last week); *Tavistock* Carnival; *Zealmpton* Show (end Jul)

August *Chagford* Agricultural and Flower Show (3rd Thur); *Dartmouth* Royal Regatta (Bank Hol weekend); *Moretonhampstead* Carnival (Bank Hol weekend); *Okehampton* Town Show; *Plymouth* Plymouth Navy Days (Bank Hol weekend) *Sidmouth* Folklore Festival (1st week); *South Molton* Annual Sheep Fair (end Aug); *Staverton* Annual Raft Race on the River Dart (end Aug)

September *Axminster* Carnival (2nd week); *Barnstaple* Three Day Fair *Bideford* Carnival and Regatta; *Newton Abbot* Cheese and Onion Fair (2nd week); *Widecombe-in-the-Moor* Widecombe Fair (2nd Tue)

October *Bampton* Livestock Fair (last Thur); *Kingsbridge* Carnival (last week); *Tavistock* Goose Fair

November *Ottery St Mary* Carnival and Tar Barrel Rolling (Nov 5)

Walks

The whole of Devon is a walker's paradise. However, visitors are advised not to walk on upland *★Dartmoor* unless properly equipped with a map, compass, boots and protective clothing. The entire Devon coast is part of the *★South West Coast Path* and has superb views and good paths.

All the walks listed below are circular, but should not be undertaken without the relevant 1:50,000 OS Map. Short walks of up to 3m are described for almost all the major coastal resorts under their Gazetteer entries.

Walk 1 *Plymouth Area Coast Walk* 4B
Leave Plymouth by car on A379 and then take B3186 to Noss Mayo. Park in the village and walk W along the coast path to Gara Point. (You will see the Great Mew Stone out to sea). Continue along the cliff top (the Warren) to Warren Cottage, then follow the made-up track, across the minor road and return down the track to the village/5m

Walk 2 *Salcombe-Bolt Head Coast Walk* 4C
Park 1½m S of Salcombe in Sharpitor. Join the South West Coast Path and walk along to Bolt Head, Off Cove, Steeple Cove to Soar Mill Cove. From here a path leads NE inland to a hotel and the hamlet of Soar. At Soar take the right fork of the minor road and at the sharp corner 100yds ahead go straight on along the footpath to the hamlet of Rew (¼m). At Rew go E along the minor road to the T junction at the valley bottom and from there walk SE back to Sharpitor/5m

Walk 3 *Brixham-Berry Head Coast Walk* 4C
Park in Brixham and walk E out of the town along the coast road past the outer harbour to Berry Head (signposted). Walk out to the tip of the head with its lighthouse and then along the S side of the promontory to St Mary's Bay. From the bay it is a short walk by road to Brixham/3½m

Walk 4 *Mortehoe Coast Walk* 1A/1B
Park in Mortehoe near the inn and walk S out of the village along the road until you join the coast path going NW. Follow it to Morte Point and on to Bull Point. From the lighthouse follow the track S back to the village. This walk can be extended by going on around the coast from Bull Point to Lee Bay. From here take the track SW. Follow it until it divides; go straight on and follow footpath ½m until paths divide; take right fork and walk 1m until you meet track. Turn left (S) and return to Morthoe/6m/9m

Walk 5 *Hartland Coast Walk* 1A/2A
Park in Stoke, 2m W of Hartland Town, and walk W along the road from the church 100yds. Take the

footpath NW that goes to Dyer's Lookout along a wood and Abbey River. At the coast, walk S along the coast path to the waterfalls at Speke's Mill Mouth (2m). Follow the track inland along the river until you join the minor road. Go N ½m up the road until it turns sharp right. Continue straight on N along the track into Stoke/6m

Walk 6 *Manaton and Becky Falls, Dartmoor*   3C

Park in Manaton and walk NE along the minor road through the village. In 1m, after a steep descent, a track leads off to the right to Foxworthy. Follow it, crossing the river and walk downstream on the path which climbs through woodland into open moorland. After going through another small wood the paths diverge: take the one downhill signposted Manaton. Cross the river and walk 200yds uphill (E) until a path comes in on the left. Follow it S along the edge of the woods until you come to Becky Falls (2m). From there walk back along the road to Manaton/6m

Walk 7 *Teign Gorge and Castle Drogo, Dartmoor*   3C

Park at Fingle Bridge car park and walk W along the N bank of the river for 1½m. Opposite the footbridge across the Teign, follow the path N up the hill to the lane and go on for ¼m to the footpath on the right sign-posted 'Hunter's Path'. Follow it for ¼m, when a steep path leads N up the hill to Castle Drogo. From the castle follow its main drive E for ½m until the roads split, take the right track E to its limit. Where it ends, follow a footpath S back to the edge of the river gorge and walk back along Hunter's Path to Fingle Bridge/4m

Walk 8 (for more experienced walkers) *Warren House Inn, Hameldown Tor and Grimspound, Dartmoor*   3B/3C

Park at *The Warren House Inn* on B3212, 2m NE of Postbridge. 100yds NE of the inn, on the other side of the road, follow the old mining track SE past the disused mines, down the river to Soussons Down Forest. Leave the track by continuing S along the river on the footpath, and around

Challacombe Down hill. The path meets a bridleway; turn left and in 300 yds, after passing a farm, cross the road and strike up Hameldown Ridge, (500ft climb; no path). Walk N along the ridge to the triangulation point at Hameldown Tor (1735ft) and on to Grimspound. From here take the path W down to the road. Walk back S down the road 100yds to the track going NW and along it to the buildings at its end. From here follow the path W, past the disused mines to the river, then follow the track back to the inn/8m

Walk 9 *Molland, Exmoor*   1C

Park in Molland and walk E along the minor road, past the T junction (chapel), past a steep dip to a track leading N onto Exmoor. In ½m take the right fork to Smallacombe, follow the track, and then the path over the moor to the minor (unfenced) road; walk E along it to Anstey Gate and take the track S ½m to the T junction of tracks. Turn right and after 100yds take the S path downhill. Cross the stream and follow the path SW to Gourte Farm. From here walk back to the road and along it (turning right at Stone) into Molland/7m

Walk 10 *Bickleigh N of Exeter*   2C

Park near the intersection of A396 and A3072. Walk ½m NW on the minor road to Cadeleigh and where the road climbs sharply take the track on the right N along the Dart river valley. Cross the first minor road (1½m) and the second (½m) and continue until you come to a third road (another 1m). Here take the track immediately to your left (on the same side of the road) to Well Town. From here follow the footpath 1m SE to Coombe, crossing a track on the way. From Coombe follow the track E to the minor road. Turn right and in 150yds left down a track which returns you to Bickleigh/7m

Walk 11 *Exeter Canal Walk*   3C/3D

An interesting industrial archeology walk. Start at the Maritime Museum and walk S down the canal along the the towpath via Countess Wear to Topsham Lock from where a ferry can be taken across the Rive Exe to Topsham (good pubs). Take a bus back to Exeter/4m

Walk 12 *Tiverton,*
Grand Western Canal   2C/2D
Park in the canal basin at Tiverton
(signposted from A373). Walk E along
the canal towpath 2m until you reach
the second road bridge over the canal,
leave the canal and walk S (right) along
the road ½m. At the T junction turn
right and walk ½m to Lower
Warnicombe Farm. There turn left
down the track and footpath through
the fields until you meet the next road.
Cross it and go W down the track to
Gogwell (½m), on past the
triangulation point (775ft), cross the
next minor road and walk 1m to the
track that runs parallel to the River
Exe. Turn right and walk back along it
into Tiverton/6m

Motoring tours

These five motoring tours take in the
best features of the county. Each is
circular and can be started at any
point. Names in brackets indicate
diversions from main route. Allow the
best part of a day for each tour.

Tour 1 *Exeter, SE coast, Honiton*
and Cullompton
Exeter – leave on Topsham Road –
Topsham – right on A376 to Exmouth
– Budleigh Salterton – East Budleigh –
right on minor road to Otterton –
Sidmouth – B3175 then right on A3052
– right on B3174 to Beer – Seaton –
B3172 to Axmouth – N on A358 –
Axminster – W on A35 to Honiton –
NW on A373 – (Hembury Fort) –
Cullompton – minor roads W to
Bickleigh – return to Exeter S on A396

Tour 2 *The English Riviera,*
Dartmouth, Kingsbridge and Totnes
Torquay – S along The Front –
Paignton – A379 – A3022 to Brixham –
B3205, A379 to River Dart (or B3205
to Kingswear) and then ferry across
River Dart to Dartmouth. Leave
Dartmouth on B3205 and left at A379
to Slapton Ley – Kingsbridge (Detour
S on A381 to Salcombe, return to
Kingsbridge) – A381 to Totnes –
Newton Abbot – Teignmouth – S
across River Teign on A379 – Shaldon
– Torquay

Tour 3 *South Dartmoor*
Plymouth – A386 to Yelverton – B3212
to Princetown – Two Bridges – B3357
to Dartmeet – left after 2m on minor
roads to Widecombe-in-the-Moor – E
along minor roads to Haytor – Haytor
Vale – Bovey Tracey – S on A382 to
A38 – (Ashburton – Buckfastleigh) –
left on B3196 and right on B3210 –
(Ugborough) – Ermington – A379 –
Yealmpton – Plymstock – Plymouth

Tour 4 *North Dartmoor*
Tavistock – E on B3357 to Two
Bridges – NE on B3212 to Postbridge
– Moretonhampstead – N on A382 –
left after 3m on minor roads to
Chagford – Gidleigh – Throwleigh –
South Zeal – A30 W to Okehampton –
A30 SW 8m then A386 – (Lydford) –
Mary Tavy – Tavistock

Tour 5 *Barnstaple, Ilfracombe*
and NW Devon
Barnstaple – SW on A39 – Instow –
Bideford – A386 to Great Torrington –
E on B3227 to Atherington –
(Chittlehampton) – South Molton – N
on A361 3m to B3226 to Brayford – to
A399 – Combe Martin – Ilfracombe –
B3231 for 5m to B3343 – W to
Woolacombe – minor road SE to
B3231 – Croyde – Braunton – A361 to
Barnstaple

Gazetteer

This includes information on the location, history and main features of the places of interest in the region. Visiting hours for all places open to the public are shown in 'The Best of the Region'. Asterisks indicate references to other Gazetteer entries

Cockington

Appledore
1A/1B

Village on A386, 3m N of Bideford

A delightful fishing, shipbuilding and sailing village on the estuaries of the Rivers Torridge and Taw, with an unspoiled quayside, old seamen's cottages in narrow winding streets and grander sea captain's houses looking out across the water.

Appledore's shipbuilding tradition goes back to Elizabethan times (ships from Appledore fought the Armada) and is maintained today. Coming down the hill from Bideford (Richmond Road) a signposted turning to the right leads to the modern *Appledore Shipyard*, built in 1969, one of the largest covered shipyards in Europe, capable of constructing two 5000-ton vessels side by side. Continuing into Appledore, the large sheds of the *Richmond Dry Dock* (1856) are on the right. This is the S end of the **Quay**: a good starting point for a walk. The Quay offers a delightful stroll, with views of Instow across the Torridge estuary, but the complex of old seamen's houses invites diversions into attractive side streets, such as Bude Street with its roof-top lookout and the Georgian Market Street. Overlooking the end of the Quay, continuing round the headland, is the Victorian *St Mary's Church*, with a sad record of those lost at sea in its churchyard.

The Quay is continued by the narrow, brightly-painted *Irsha Street*, with alleys and slipways running down to the sea. At the end is the Customs House and Lifeboat Station, and beyond *Hinks Yard*, where replicas of *The Golden Hind* and other famous old wooden ships have been made by craftsmen using original woodworking tools. The return to the Quay can be made by a footpath over Staddon Hill, site of a fort built by the local Parliamentarians in 1642 and surrendered to the Royalists a year later. The hill offers a splendid view over Bideford Bay and out to Lundy Island.

The footpath joins Staddon Road and thence the junction with Richmond Road. On the way downhill note the splendid mansion of William Yeo (*The*

28

Holt, 1856) builder of the Richmond Dock. A turning left, Odun Road, leads to the *North Devon Maritime Museum*, containing interesting ship models and photographs. *Docton House* (14th-c.) at the foot of Richmond Road, is reckoned to be the oldest house in Appledore. (Return to The Quay.)

Arlington Court (NT)   1B
Historic house off A39, 7m NE of Barnstaple

Built in 1820, Arlington is a modest Regency house with a semi-circular portico. Inside is a delightfully furnished museum reflecting the Victorian tastes of its last owner, Miss Rosalie Chichester (the aunt of Sir Francis Chichester), who gave the property to the National Trust in 1949. There are her own collections of sea-shells, musical instruments, snuff boxes, model ships, and a watercolour by William Blake, *Cycle of the Life of Man*. On the splendid central staircase is a display of dresses covering the period 1830-1910. In the stables are horse-drawn carriages, and the large park offers a nature trail and a variety of animals including Jacob sheep and Shetland ponies.

Ashburton   3C
Town on A38, 20m SW of Exeter. Event: Ale-tasting and bread-weighing ceremony (Summer Carnival week, end Jun). EC Wed MD Tue

A really charming and unspoiled market town on the SE of Dartmoor, Ashburton is one of Devon's four ancient Stannary towns, concerned with the control of tin-mining. Among the delightful houses, many dating back to the 17th c., is the *House of Cards* (now the International Store) in North Street, with playing card motifs picked out on the tile-hung front. In West Street, the town's main street, there is a small but interesting *Museum* in a former brush factory, specialising in local history and American-Indian antiquities. **St Andrew's Church** (off West Street) is built of Devon limestone and granite and has an impressive tower (92ft). Another 14th-c. building is *St Lawrence Chapel* (St Lawrence Street), which

served as the local grammar school before the last war. Only the tower remains of the original building: the rest is late 16th-c.

For refreshment visitors are well served. At one end of the town is *The Golden Lion Inn* (1820), – a fascinating coaching inn noted for its food – and at the other end *The Exeter Inn*, built as a private house opposite the church. Between them is the interesting old *London Inn* and many excellent old-world tea-rooms with tempting Devonshire cream teas.

4m NW on the B3357 at *New Bridge* there is a National Park Information Centre.

Ashcombe   3C
Village off A380, 10m S of Exeter

Situated at the foot of two very steep roads on Dawlish Water, Ashcombe has a charming woodland position. **St Nectan's Church**, built in the 13th c., retains its original tower, but the rest of the building was revamped 1824-5 and is now a delicate 'Gothick', though fortunately the 15th-c. bench ends remain. Adjacent to it is the enchanting early 19th-c. *Vicarage* with veranda. 1m NE is *Mamhead Obelisk* (1742), intended as a guide to ships at sea.

Aveton Gifford   4B
Village on A379, 4m NW of Kingsbridge

A traditional one-street Devon village, noteworthy for its 13th-c **St Andrew's Church**, badly damaged during the war, which nestles beside a large medieval farm. There is a wonderful walk along the river estuary, with its mudflats teeming with bird life. A medieval bridge, 1200ft long, spans the river S of the village.

Axminster   4D
Small town on A35, 10m E of Honiton. Event: Carnival (2nd week in Sep). EC Wed MD Thur. Inf: Tel (0297) 34386

Attractive hill town on the River Axe, famous for its carpets. Established here in 1755, the industry later (1835), moved to Wilton in Salisbury, now equally famous for its carpets. In 1937, however, carpet-making was revived with the opening of a new factory, *Axminster Carpets*, which offers conducted tours (see *Industrial & Rural Heritage*, p.20). Axminster itself is of great antiquity, being at the intersection of two ancient roads, the Icknield Way and Fosse Way. It remains an amiable undeveloped town, with pleasant 18th- and 19th-c. shop frontages. At the SW end are the fragmentary ruins of *Newenham Abbey*. There is trout fishing in the Axe.

Axmouth
4D

Village on B3172, 7m S of Axminster

A beautifully sited one-street village nestling in the valley where a branch of the old Fosse Way meets the River Axe. The Norman **St Michael's Church** was built for a larger congregation than the village can now muster. Both the church and 800-year-old *Harbour Inn* are reminders that Axmouth was once a port of consequence – until the Axe silted up in the 12th c. It now has the feeling of a lost village, and there are marvellous walks hereabouts.

To the S of the village is a golf course and the *Dowlands Cliffs*, now a nature reserve. The cliffs have always been subject to slippage and in 1839 millions of tons came away (which the villagers thought presaged the end of the world), forming the present dramatic chasms.

Bampton
2D

Small town on A361 & A396, 6m N of Tiverton. Event: Livestock Fair (last Thur in Oct). EC Thur

A lovely market town with some stylish Georgian houses just S of Exmoor, Bampton once had a castle, much fought over in King Stephen's reign. Only the *Motte* (or mound on which it stood) now remains at the N end of the town. Originally Norman, the **Church of St Michael and All Angels** was rebuilt in the 15th-16th c. and restored in the late 19th c. The rood screen survives from the 15th c., though it lost its upper section through mutilation during the Reformation. In the churchyard are two venerable yews, thought to be 500 years old. The town is

a centre of hunting and hacking, with trout fishing on the Exe. The major annual event is the fair of Exmoor ponies, which takes place in October.

1½m SW is the *Chain Bridge*, an early iron bridge over the River Exe.

Bantham
4B

Village off A379, 7m W of Kingsbridge

Reached only by winding lanes wide enough for one car, this tiny settlement boasts superb sandy beaches on the estuary of the River Avon. There are breathtaking walks along the coast to *Thurlestone*. The swimming is excellent, though the currents can be difficult at times.

Barnstaple
1B

Pop 17,820. 40m NW of Exeter (A377). Event: Three Day Fair (Sep). EC Wed MD Tue & Fri. Inf: Tel (0271) 72742

Barnstaple claims to be the oldest borough in Britain, traditionally granted its charter in 930. The earliest form of the name of the town was 'Beardastapol' ('stapol' meaning pillar or market). During the Elizabethan period it had its own theatre and Shakespeare is supposed to have acted here. One of the striking features of the town is the 13th- c. 16-arch *bridge* across the River Taw. Until the silting-up of the Taw estuary in the 19th c., Barnstaple was a thriving seaport: it is now predominantly a market town.

Starting from the bridge, on the N side of the river in *The Square* is the *North Devon Athenaeum*, a private library and small museum founded in 1888. To the SE, in Litchdon Street, are some fine 17th-c. *Almshouses*, consisting of 20 cottages facing a pretty inner courtyard (open to the public).

From The Square, walk along the *High Street*, in which most of the shops are Georgian. On the right, reached through an alley, is the 14th-c. **St Peter's Church** with its famous crooked lead-covered spire of 1676. Beyond it in Paternoster Row is the 14th-c. **St Anne's Chapel.** First a chantry chapel, this was later the grammar school and is now a *museum* of local history and antiques. Between the church and the chapel an alley leads into **Butcher's Row**, a delightful arcade of stalls erected in 1855. Opposite is the late Victorian *Pannier Market*, which comes to life on market days. At the E end of the Pannier Market is the *Queen's Hall*, and at the W end the Georgian *Guildhall*. In the High Street opposite is *The Three Tuns Tavern* of 1450, with its fine oak panelling and beamed ceilings.

The next turning on the left off the High Street is Holland Walk, a pleasant, if short, shopping parade. Down Holland Street, the Cattle Market is passed on the right and behind it the *Castle Mound*. Turn left into Castle Street and walk along the Strand to the colonnaded arcade of **Queen Ann's Walk** (1708), a meeting place for trade. The *Tome Stone*, on which merchants placed their money to seal a bargain, can still be seen. From the arcade it is a short walk back to the bridge.

On the opposite side of the river by the bridge is the *North Devon Leisure Centre* with swimming pools, games rooms and other sports facilities.

Beaford 2B
Village on B3220, 8m SE of Great Torrington

Housing a branch of the *Dartington Hall* complex, Beaford is a centre of craft instruction and travelling theatre groups, with various fringe activities throughout the year.

The *Beaford Pottery* at the Old Parsonage is open to visitors during usual shop hours.

Becky Falls 3C
Dartmoor waterfall on B3344, 4m S of Moretonhampstead

Perfectly situated in more than 50 acres of luxuriant woodland, Becky Falls is a splendid series of waterfalls dropping 70ft. The falls, which are particularly dramatic after rainfall, are close to the road (ample parking space). A beautiful circular walk of 8m, starting from *Manaton*, takes in the falls, going through lushest Dartmoor. (See *Walk 6*, p.26.)

Beer 4D
Village on S coast (B3174), 1m W of Seaton and 22m SE of Exeter

A lovely traditional fishing and smuggling village overlooked by high chalk cliffs honeycombed with caves, and with a stream running down the main street. Beer was once famous for its lace, and the lace for Queen Victoria's wedding dress was made here. It was also a quarrying centre from Roman times, and the stone from Beer built Exeter Cathedral. In the village is the *Axe Vale and Beer Pottery* which specialises in hand-decorated work (open to the public weekdays 10-12 & 2-4), and on the hillside above the village at *Beer Modelrama* runs the *Beer Heights Light Railway*, where there is also a museum of model railways.

At low tide there is a charming walk E along the beach to *Seaton*, or W along the cliffs (*South West Coast Path*) over *Beer Head* (426ft, the most westerly outpost of chalk in England) towards *Branscombe* and *Sidmouth* (9m). 1m NW of the village is *Bovey House* (1592), now a hotel, with fine Jacobean carving. It was used as a store and meeting place by smugglers in the 18th c.

Berry Head 4C
Coastal promontory 2m E of A3022, 1m E of Brixham

This promontory is known for superb cliff walks and panoramic views of Torbay, and in clear weather towards the Dorset Coast and Portland Bill. Originally the site of an Iron Age settlement, the Romans used Berry Head as a look-out post and numerous archeological remains have been found in caverns used by the soldiers for refuse. There are the remains of polygonal defences built against a Napoleonic invasion, and one of the smallest lighthouses in England, only 10ft tall and 191ft above sea level. In 1814, while awaiting exile to the Isle of Elba, Napoleon was kept in a ship moored off Berry Head. This was the closest he ever got to England.

There is a 3½m walk from Brixham around the head (see *Walk 3*, p.25).

Berrynarbor 1B
Village off A399, 4m E of Ilfracombe

Situated in rolling countryside a short walk from the sea, Berrynarbor is a charming village with an interesting *Manor House* built in the reign of Edward IV and now the Village Institute. On the way to ★*Combe Martin* is *Ye Olde Globe*, an historic and charming inn with old beams. On the coast is ★*Watermouth Castle*, a popular tourist attraction.

Berry Pomeroy Castle 4C
Castle off A381, 2m E of Totnes, ¾m N of Berry Pomeroy village

One of the most imposing castles in the south-west, situated on the edge of a ravine in dense woodland. Built by the Norman de la Pomerai family (later Pomeroy) *c.* 1300, the castle was sold to Edward Seymour, the Lord Protector Somerset, in 1548. Now ruined, the castle retains its original outer shell and the remains of a vast Tudor mansion of the Seymours, never completed. The reason for the castle's ruin has never been explained: its air of mystery is enhanced by stories that it is haunted by the ghost of Lady Margaret Pomeroy. The castle is served by a café and car park.

In the village of *Berry Pomeroy* 1m S, the 15th-c. **St Mary's Church** has an exceptional screen of superb craftsmanship and the tombs of the Pomeroy and Seymour families who built the castle.

Bickleigh 2C
Village and historic house on A396, 3m S of Tiverton

A delightful village of colour-washed thatched cottages on the River Exe, with a 14th-c. church, historic pub (*The Trout Inn*), and a fortified manor house. The *Bickleigh Mill Craft Centre and Farm* is a fascinating complex including a restored watermill where craftsmen can be seen at work, farm activities and animals, a fish farm and an agricultural crafts museum.

Bickleigh Castle, ½m down-river, has a 900-year history. A Norman castle

which originally stood on the site was destroyed by King Stephen: only the 11th-c. chapel survives. The Tudor castle which replaced it was itself largely destroyed in the Civil War: all that remains of this is the gatehouse (through which the gardens are entered) and the S wing. The N wing was rebuilt as a cob and thatch farmhouse after the Restoration.

In the surviving parts of the castle (restored in this century) which include the Great Hall, Guard Room, Armoury, etc. is a good collection of furniture and armour. The **Chapel**, built between 1090 and 1110, is thought to be the oldest building in Devon.

A delightful circular walk of 7m along the upper reaches of the River Dart starts in the village (see *Walk 10*, p.26).

Bicton Gardens 3D
Gardens on A376, 3m N of Budleigh Salterton

It comes as a surprise to find a formal 18th-c. garden in Devon, similar to those of 17th-c. France. The most spectacular feature of the gardens is the avenue of monkey puzzle trees, but there are also a tropical house, cacti house, pinetum, fountains, terraces and lawns.

Bicton House, a plain Georgian building of 1730, remodelled 1908, was the home of the Barons Rolle of Stevenstone. It is now an agricultural college. Within the estate are two churches: one a romantic medieval ruin, the other 1851. Of the same date is the *Rolle Mausoleum*, designed by Pugin, which contains the impressive marble tomb of Denys Rolle (1638). An additional attraction is the *Country Life and Transport Museum*, with a narrow-gauge railway and rides on vintage buses.

Bideford 1A
Pop 12,610. 9m SW of Barnstaple (A39). Events: Carnival and Regatta (Sep). EC Wed MD Tue & Sat. Inf: Tel (02372) 77676

Once one of Britain's major ports, Bideford's heyday was from the late 16th to mid-18th c. The great Elizabethan sea captain Sir Richard Grenville sailed from here in *The Revenge* to fight the Spaniards off the Azores in 1591,

Crafts

and his family have long been associated with the town.

A magnificent medieval 24-arch bridge, 667ft long, spans the River Torridge, and the tree-lined **Quay** and adjacent streets are rich in old buildings. Bideford has had a market since 1272, and in the 17th c. it had a valuable trade in tobacco with Virginia (the warehouses are there today), as well as wool and timber. To the W of the Quay is *Bridgeland Street*, laid out in 1690, which still has many of the original merchants' houses.

At the N end of the Quay is *Victoria Park*, with eight ancient guns from the Spanish Armada and facilities for bathing, putting, tennis and a children's playground. The *Burton Art Gallery* in the park contains painting, pottery and local items.

On the other side of the bridge is *East-the-Water*, where *The Royal Hotel* (1688) has a splendid plaster ceiling. Charles Kingsley lived here from 1854, and made the area famous with his novel *Westward Ho!* in which much of the action centres around Bideford. There is rowing and sailing on the River Torridge, as well as trout fishing.

Bigbury-on-Sea
See *Burgh Island*

Bishopsteignton   3C
Town on River Teign and A381, 4m NE of Newton Abbot

An unspoiled town with narrow streets and an air of bustle. The impressive **St John's Church** has a Norman doorway complete with dog-tooth and zig-zag patterns, and built into the S wall is an oddly primitive relief carving of the Three Wise Men and the Virgin Mary.

Blackbury Castle   3D
Ancient site nr Southleigh off B3174, 5m NW of Seaton

An oval-shaped Iron Age fort with a bank and ditch. It has a complicated entrance, designed to confuse attackers. The fort is now under the protection of the Department of the Environment, and is a good spot for a picnic. 1m N is *Farway Countryside Park*.

Bolt Head and **Bolt Tail**
See *Salcombe*

Bovey Tracey   3C
Small town on A382, 6m NW of Newton Abbot.
EC Wed. Inf: Tel (0626) 832047. Nat Park HQ Inf:
Tel (0626) 832093

A pleasant, mainly brick town on a steep hill on the edge of Dartmoor, Bovey's tourist information office and excellent inn make it a natural starting point for a tour of the region. There is an old watermill in the town, and a bridge of 1643. The 15th-c. **Church of St Thomas of Canterbury** has some fine monuments in stone and alabaster and elaborately carved screen and pulpit (both early 15th-c.).

¾m W off the B3344 is *Parke*, a classical mansion of 1820 in its own parkland which houses the head-quarters of the *National Parks Service*. There is an information and enquiries office in the house which is open during office hours all year.

Yarner Wood Nature Reserve, 2m W by the B3344, contains two well-laid-out woodland walks, one of 1½m and the other 3¼m, with information boards throughout. 1½m away on the Haytor Road is the *David Leach Pottery*, open during normal shop hours. David Leach is the son of the world-famous potter Bernard Leach.

Branscombe   4D
Village on S coast off A3052, 6m E of Sidmouth

An exceptionally lovely straggling village with cob and thatch cottages in a steep woody valley. **St Winifred's Church** is in a sheltered position and is imposing for such a small place. It has a broad Norman tower, a three-decker pulpit and Elizabethan gallery (both rare in Devon), box pews and fine monuments. The only access to the gallery is up steps outside the church, an arrangement so inconvenient for the communicants that it is found in no other church in the country. *Church Living*, opposite the church, is an unusually shaped medieval cottage, said to have a complete house hidden away below it. The *Old Forge* at the bottom of

Buckland Abbey

Portrait of Drake, Drake's Drum and model of Golden Hind   Opposite: Clovelly

the valley has been in continuous use since 1580, and ¼m N is *The Mason's Arms*, an excellent and ancient inn. ½m S is *Branscombe Mouth*, a pebbly beach where fossils are sometimes found. On either side are sheer cliffs, owned by the NT, that offer outstanding cliff-top walks, part of the **South West Coast Path*.

Braunton 1B

Village on A361, 5m NW of Barnstaple

Despite its population of 6406, Braunton is still officially classified as a village. **St Brannock's Church** is one of the finest in the county. St Brannock was a wandering Celtic missionary who founded a minster here in the 6th c. He is buried under the altar. The existing building dates from the 13th c. and has a fine Norman tower and spire over the S transept: an unusual site for a tower. Inside, the chestnut benches have finely carved ends and the Lady Chapel a handsome Portuguese chest, believed to have come from the Spanish Armada. Behind the church is the *Braunton and District Museum*, which contains a good deal of interesting local material, and SW is the 350-acre *Braunton Great Field*, a rare survival of Saxon strip farming.

2m SW of the village are the celebrated **Braunton Burrows**, a great expanse of sand dunes, with a lighthouse at the S tip, supporting rare plants and birds (sometimes closed for army firing practice). Part of the Burrows is a National Nature Reserve (access permitted). Beyond are *Saunton Golf Course* and *Saunton Sands*, a magnificent 3m-long sandy beach.

Church

Brixham 4C

Pop 12,000. 10m S of Torquay (A379). EC Wed. Inf: Tel (08045) 2861

Brixham is one of the busiest working ports on the S coast, and the **harbour** is a hive of colourful activity. Fish can be bought as it is landed at the *Fish Market* on the quay, boats can be hired and there is a passenger ferry in the summer across Tor Bay to **Torquay*. Fishing trips are always available.

The town is in two halves. The older part, Upper Brixham, has the parish *Church of St Mary*, originally Saxon and mainly 15th-c. The church in the lower town, *All Saints*', is known for its early 19th-c. vicar, Henry Lyte, who wrote *Abide With Me* and other well-known hymns.

In 1588 one of the flagships of the Spanish Armada was captured at sea and brought into Brixham harbour as plunder. Exactly 100 years later the 'Glorious' or 'Bloodless Revolution' started when William of Orange landed here on his way to London to take the throne from the last Stuart king. A *statue* to him on the quay commemorates the event.

The town has much to attract visitors, including a full-size replica of Sir Francis Drake's *Golden Hind* afloat in the harbour and the *Marine Aquarium and Trawling Exhibition* on the quay. The *Brixham Museum* at Bolton Cross at the top end of Fore Street incorporates the National Coastguard museum and includes sections on fishing, lifeboats, and boatbuilding. *Brixham Pottery* (Milton Street), open during normal shop hours, is well worth a visit.

There is a beach with good swimming at *St Mary's Bay* on the S side of the town. 1m E is **Berry Head*, famous for its views of Torbay; there is a circular walk to it from the town. (see *Walk 3*, p.25.)

Broadclyst 2D

Village on B3181, 5m NE of Exeter

A pleasant village untouched by its proximity to Exeter, with an impressive 15th-c. *Church* surrounded by clipped yews. The church has fine carvings and a number of spectacular monuments. The one to Sir John Acland, lying on his tomb, life size and in full armour, is one of the most sumptuous in Devon. 2m N is **Killerton House and Gardens*.

Broadhembury 2D

Village off A373, 5m NW of Honiton

Considered the best example of a thatched village in the West Country. The colour-washed cottages are grouped around a square, with a large 14th-c. *Church* dominating the scene. The author of the hymn *Rock of Ages* was vicar here in the late 18th c. W of the churchyard is the 15th-c. *Priest's House*. The *Drewe Arms* is as old as the church and may have been the Church House before becoming an ale house. 2m SE on the A373 is Hembury Fort (see **Honiton*).

Buckfastleigh & Buckfast Abbey　3C
Town and abbey on A38, 23m SW of Exeter
EC Wed

Buckfastleigh is a rather faded town, once prosperous on account of its large woollen mill (now disused), but not unattractive. Above the town to the E, and rather desolate, is the 13th-c. **Church of the Holy Trinity**. In its churchyard are the ruins of a 13th-c. chantry chapel and the tomb of Sir Richard Cabell, an evil man who lived in the 17th c. and on whose death black dogs raced across the moor to howl at his corpse (a legend that fed Sir Arthur Conan Doyle's imagination when he wrote *The Hound of the Baskervilles*).

Buckfastleigh is the starting point of the **Dart Valley Railway*, in the grounds of which is the passenger-carrying *Riverside Miniature Railway*.

1m E is *Buckfast*, which hardly exists apart from its internationally famous **Abbey**. Founded in 1018 and later destroyed, the abbey was rebuilt from scratch by the French Benedictine monks who had bought the site in 1882. Most of the work was carried out (1906-32) by the monks themselves, with never more than six working at a time – a remarkable achievement considering the scale of the building.

Built in the local stone, the abbey is basically Norman in style, and somewhat ponderous. There are, however, redeeming features such as the stained glass, designed and made by the monks. The Buckfast Abbey bees are famous, and honey is on sale to visitors, as is the abbey's tonic wine. A further attraction is the *Museum of Shellcraft*, where painted, engraved and carved shells are on display.

Buckland Abbey (NT)　3B
Historic house 2m W of A386, 5m S of Tavistock

Founded in 1278 as a Cistercian abbey, Buckland Abbey became an irregular Elizabethan house after the Reformation. It was associated with two famous Elizabethan seafarers: first Sir Richard Grenville, who converted the church into a three-storied manor in the 1570s, and later Sir Francis Drake, who bought the property in 1581 with the proceeds of his voyage round the world. The combination of church and manor can be seen in many details. Most conspicuous is the *Banqueting Hall*, with its fine plaster ceiling, which was the original nave, and the surviving church tower, a massive block over the crossing. Some alterations to the house were carried out in the 1770s, when the main staircase was added, and again in 1937 after the building was severely damaged by fire. Much of the house is now a naval museum, with Grenville and Drake relics (including the famous Drake's Drum) and is administered by the Plymouth Corporation for the National Trust, who acquired the property in 1948.

In the grounds there is a 14th-c. *Tithe Barn*, 180ft long, containing an interesting range of horse-drawn vehicles. The old abbey gatehouse has been incorporated in the stables. The gardens have many fine shrubs.

1m N in the village of *Buckland Monachorum*, the *Church* (15th-c.) has a hammerbeam roof with carved angels. It has many Drake associations, with its Drake Aisle crammed with monuments. The *Drake Manor* inn was once the Church House.

Buckland-in-the-Moor　3C
Dartmoor village off B3357, 4m NW of Ashburton

A village of immense natural charm, with its pretty thatched cottages, richly scented gardens, tree-shadowed lanes, and miniature cascades of water. Secluded behind their garden walls are many fine country houses, including the Georgian *Buckland Court*. The 14th-c. **St Peter's Church**, with its fine screen and paintings, has a unique

Buckland-in-the-Moor

clock, marked with the words M-Y-D-E-A-R-M-O-T-H-E-R instead of the hours.

1m E is *Buckland Beacon* (390ft) with magnificent views S. Near its summit are the *Ten Commandment Stones*, two flat rocks carved with the sacred texts by a local craftsman.

Buckland Monachorum
See *Buckland Abbey*

Budleigh Salterton   3D
Town on A376, 4m E of Exmouth. Event: Gala Week (Spring Bank Hol). EC Thur. Inf: Tel (03954) 5275

An enchanting little seaside town with Regency-style shops, fine panoramic views, a little stream that runs along the main street, masses of flowers, and an air of elegance, reflected by the well-mannered early 19th-c. cottages. On Saturdays and Sundays lace-makers ply their craft for the benefit of visitors.

The beach is famous for its oval pebbles, depicted in Millais's painting *The Boyhood of Raleigh* (Tate Gallery, London) which shows the great seafarer as a child sitting before a sea wall that still exists. The town is the headquarters of the East Devon Golf Club; and the Lawn Tennis & Croquet Club has a national reputation that reflects the 'classy' character of the town. The delightful *Fairlynch Museum* in Fore Street has a smuggler's cellar and a special section on Sir Walter Raleigh, who grew up in the area. There are bracing walks along the cliff-top to *Exmouth*, and the estuary of the River Otter is a favourite area for birdwatchers.

2m N is **East Budleigh**, a delightful old village with a notable 15th-c. *Church* used by Raleigh and with wonderful, almost pagan, carved bench ends. 1m E of this village is *Hayes Barton*, the medieval farmhouse where Raleigh was born in 1552 (not open to the public).

3m N of Budleigh Salterton are the beautiful *Bicton Gardens*, and 1m E of them is *Otterton Mill*, a working watermill mentioned in the Domesday Book. The mill has an exhibition gallery and lace-making display.

Burgh Island 4B
Island on S coast nr Bigbury-on-Sea off B3392, 6m
W of Kingsbridge

300 yds out in the mouth of the River
Avon, this small island can be walked to
at low tide, but at other times there is a
curious vehicle on stilts, the 'Sea
Tractor' to convey visitors across. The
island provides a striking setting for *The
Pilchard Inn* (1336), an old smugglers'
haunt.

The neighbouring seaside village of
Bigbury-on-Sea has a golf course and
fine sand bars which offer safe bathing.

Burrator Reservoir
see *Sheepstor*

Cadhay House 2D
Historic house on B3176, 1m N of Ottery St Mary,
11m E of Exeter

This house has an 18th-c. front but is
basically Tudor, built by John Haydon
c. 1550 with stones acquired from the
Ottery College of Priests following the
Dissolution. The building surrounds an
open court. The inner walls of the
courtyard are attractively faced with
flint and stone and there are four quaint
statues of Henry VIII and his three
children, carved in 1617. In 1736 the
house was sold to William Peere
Williams, who added the entrance front
and divided the *Great Hall* into two
storeys. The Tudor fireplace and part of
the hammerbeam roof survive this
modification. The *Long Gallery* contains a collection of marine paintings
and pewter.

Castle Drogo (NT) 3C
Historic house off A382, 5m NW of
Moretonhampstead

A massive granite castle built between
1910 and 1930 by Sir Edwin Lutyens for
Julius Drewe, Castle Drogo is the
last great private house to be built on
such a scale in Britain. Drewe, founder
of the Home and Colonial stores, had
retired at the age of 33 and decided to
spend the rest of his life in grandeur.
Related distantly to the Norman Drogo
or Dru family (whose name survives in
nearby Drewsteignton) he chose a site
near the village, commanding the River

Teign, to build his medieval-style
castle, which one might think more
suited to a feudal baron than a 20th-c.
entrepreneur. The bare granite (of the
interior as well as the exterior) is
somewhat forbidding, but visitors can
only marvel at the daring of both patron
and architect, who shared the same
romantic concept.

The Drewe family still occupy the
upper part of the house, but visitors can
explore the ground floor and basement.
The bare walls, huge granite arches,
timber beams and tapestries maintain
the austere splendour of another age.

There is 4m circular walk along the
Teign Gorge and past the castle. (See
Walk 7, p.26.)

Chagford 3B
Small town off A382, 5m NW of
Moretonhampstead. Event: Agricultural & Flower
Show (3rd Thur in Aug). EC Wed

Despite its former importance as one of
the four ancient Stannary towns of
Devon (involved in the stamping,
weighing and assaying of tin), Chagford is reached only by a network
of narrow lanes, and it is something of a
surprise to come across this enchanting
town of thatched colour-washed cottages on the rural edge of Dartmoor.

In the centre of the market square is
the medieval *Market Cross*, with
diminutive shops on four sides. **St
Michael's Church** (consecrated 1261)
is massive for the size of the town (pop.
1250). Inside, all the pillars are hewn
from single blocks of granite, and there
are a number of good monuments
including a curious one of 1575 with
mermen and mermaids. The churchyard is very large – showing that the
town was once bigger and that this is an
area of rural depopulation. Facing the
church is the granite *Three Crowns
Hotel*, early Tudor with mullioned
windows and a grand two-storeyed
porch. To the NW of the town over the
lovely River Teign is a 16th-c. bridge,
and all around is excellent walking. 2m
NW are the delightful villages of
Gidleigh and *Throwleigh*, and 4m SW
is *Fernworthy Reservoir*. 3m E down-
river is the remarkable *Castle Drogo*.

Chambercombe Manor 1B
Historic house off B3230, 1m SE of Ilfracombe

A charming old manor house, originally belonging to the Champernowne family (12th-15th-c.). The present buildings are 16th-17th-c., with eight rooms showing furniture of the period. The whitewashed buildings, grouped round a courtyard, are situated in delightful 2-acre grounds with an Elizabethan herb garden, water garden and peacocks. In the tradition of the best old West Country houses, Chambercombe has its mystery. In the last century a skeleton was discovered bricked up in a secret chamber: believed to be that of Kate Oatway, the daughter of a wrecker. How or why she met her fate is not known, but her shade lingers on in 'the haunted chamber'.

Chudleigh 3C
Small town on A38, 12m S of Exeter. EC Wed

A quiet country town, Chudleigh rose from the ashes after a devastating fire in 1807. There are innumerable Regency houses of quality set along the old coaching road, and on the outskirts of the town are The Rock Gardens, an attractive commercial nursery. Behind the gardens rises *Chudleigh Rocks*, an imposing mass of limestone, popular for picnic parties of the type that Jane Austen enjoyed in the 18th c., but now private land. To the SE is the Iron Age hill fort known as *Castle Dyke*. On the road S (leading to *Ugbrooke House*) is *The Wheel*, a well-restored mill open as a *Craft Centre* and tearooms.

Clovelly 1A
Village on N coast off A39 (B3237), 12m W of Bideford

This famous and unique village is best approached from the E via **Hobby Drive** (entrance ½m W of Bucks Cross on A39), a romantic scenic route created as a hobby in the last century by the owner of the land. It is wooded and has enchanting views. (Weekdays in season only, small charge).

Clovelly is a picture-postcard village based on a steep and narrow street lined with colour-washed thatched cottages.

Valley of the Rocks

There is no transport up and down this street except for donkeys and sleds carrying goods. Even beer and the post is delivered by donkey. At the foot of the village is the 16th-c. pier and a tiny harbour, the only shelter for many miles on this rugged coast.

¼m outside the village on the B3237 is the charming old **All Saints' Church**, 15th-c. but on Saxon foundations. The outer doorway of the S porch is Norman, so too the embattled W tower. Inside the church are fine monuments to the Cary family, lords of the manor until 1724. Adjacent is *Clovelly Court* (1789) from where a path leads to the *Gallantry Bower* (¾m), 387ft high, an almost sheer cliff with glorious views towards Lundy Island, Braunton and Bideford. Clovelly was popularised by Charles Kingsley (whose father was rector here) and Charles Dickens, and although visited by tens of thousands of people every year it remains unspoiled.

1m S, close to the turn-off from the A39, are the *Clovelly Dykes*, three Iron Age encampments, from which there are splendid views.

Cockington 4C
Village in Torbay, off A379, 3m W of Torquay

A likely candidate for the most-photographed village in England, Cockington retains its charm, even though it has been overwhelmed by Torbay. No part of Cockington is particularly old, as much of it was moved by the lord of the manor when it spoiled the view from Cockington Court. The thatched *Old Forge* is the focal point of the village, and *The Drum Inn* (1934, Sir Edwin Lutyens), lofty and thatched, is well worth a visit.

The Elizabethan **Cockington Court** (classicized in Georgian times), is owned by Torbay council (along with the rest of the village) and contains a café; its gardens and sunken lakes are delightfully laid out. In its park stands the lovely 14th-15th-c. parish *Church* which has an interesting pulpit and fine wooden screen. Nearby is *Compton Castle*, as well as the pleasures of *Torquay* and *Paignton*.

Colyton 4D
Village on B3161, 7m SW of Axminster

Quiet and undisturbed, Colyton dates back to Saxon times. The Norman **St Andrew's Church** has an unusual crossing tower (12th-14th-c.) with an octagonal lantern added in the 15th c. when the village had enhanced its prosperity with the wool trade. Inside are fragments of a curious Saxon cross found after a disastrous fire in 1933, and a number of monuments to the Pole family. Parts of the *Vicarage* nearby go back to 1529, and many of the cottages, such as the *Old Church House* and *Great House* are not much later. The modest *Congregational Chapel* is well worth a look; it was built in 1814. A ride on the world's only surviving open-top tram may be taken to the sea-side town of *Seaton*.

Combe Martin 1B
Village on N coast (A399), 5m E of Ilfracombe

The village, straggling for 1½m in the valley of the River Umber, came into existence with the discovery of silver here in the 14th c. It is now a popular seaside resort with small intimate beaches. It is surrounded by splendid National Trust land, with exciting footpaths to the headlands of *Little Hangman* and *Great Hangman* and on to the secluded beach at the mouth of the River Heddon (7m).

In the village, the 15th-c **Church of St Peter ad Vincula** has a 100ft tower and beautiful chancel and nave. It also has the only rood screen in N Devon retaining its original panel paintings (15th-c.). A fascinating inn is the 18th-c. *Pack of Cards*. Built like a child's card house – on the winnings from gambling – it has four floors and a curious array of eight grouped chimneys and 52 windows.

A lonely chimney to the NE of the village is the only visible relic of mining activity, but Combe Martin's silver mines were once so important that the village had its own market (from 1264). The City of London has an Elizabethan cup made from Combe Martin silver weighing 136 oz.

On the E outskirts is *Buzzacott Manor*, which has a Woolly Monkey Park with a breeding group. There are also children's entertainments and a garden centre. At *Higher Leigh Manor* 1m SE of the village (A399), is another Monkey Sanctuary, where the monkeys roam freely among visitors (other attractions are the gardens and a model railway). 1½m W on the A399 is *Watermouth Castle*.

Compton Castle (NT) 3C
Historic house off A3022, 5m W of Torquay

One of the finest medieval fortified manor houses in the country, Compton Castle has an unforgettable front of towers, battlements and buttresses (*c.* 1530) which hides the 14th-c. house. The house has long been associated with the Gilbert family, most notably the Elizabethan explorer Sir Humphrey Gilbert, who sailed from Plymouth to Newfoundland in 1583 to set up one of the first English colonies in America. Only a small part of the interior is open to the public: these rooms include the chapel and 16th-c. kitchen.

Countisbury 1C
Village on A39, 2m E of Lynton

1000ft up, and ¼m from the cliff, Countisbury is at the top of the 1:4 hill into Lynmouth. The village is little more than a church and (excellent) inn, but makes a good centre for cliff walks. ¼m SW of the village is *Countisbury Camp*, an ancient fort with ditch and ramparts. 1½m N, overlooking the Bristol Channel, is *Foreland Point* with its lighthouse.

Cranmere Pool, Dartmoor 3B
Pool in centre of Dartmoor. No road access. 6m S of Okehampton, 10m W of Moretonhampstead

A sinister bog, the improbable source of the Rivers Dart, Tavy and Teign, and inspiration for the setting of Sir Arthur Conan Doyle's *The Hound of the Baskervilles*. The ghost of Benjamin Gayer, once a mayor of Okehampton, is said to haunt the pool in the form of a black pony. The pool is almost in the dead centre of Dartmoor, and is

probably best approached from *Fernworthy Reservoir* or *Okehampton*. It is not an easy stroll and those who seek it should be properly equipped with a large-scale map and compass. It is also in a military training zone, so watch out for red flags indicating the use of live ammunition.

Crediton 2C
Town on A377, 8m NW of Exeter. Event: Great Market (3rd Sat in Apr). EC Wed

Claimed as the birthplace of St Boniface (7th c. AD), Crediton became the bishopric of Devon and Cornwall until 1050, when in the face of a Danish invasion it was moved to Exeter. The historic town was unhappily all but destroyed by four disastrous fires between 1743 and 1772, and most of the old part is now either Georgian or Victorian.

The pride of the town is now the cathedral-size **Holy Cross Church**. The red sandstone building dates from the 11th c., but was enlarged in 1413 with an impressive central tower, glorious E and W windows and a Lady Chapel (*c.* 1300), that was used as the grammar school until 1860. There are some fine tombs. Next to the church, the 13th-c. *Chapter House* contains a Civil War armoury.

Croyde 1A
Village on N coast (B3231), 10m NW of Barnstaple

A pretty village with excellent surfing facilities and beaches of the rock-pool-and-seaweed variety. The popular *Croyde Gem, Rock and Shell Museum* has a collection of rough-cut and polished gems and shells from all over the world.

1m NW is *Baggy Point*, a 400ft promontory with marvellous views which separates Croyde Bay from *Woolacombe Bay*. To the S is the great expanse of *Saunton Sands* and *Braunton Burrows*.

Cullompton 2D
Small town on M5 (Exit 28) and B3181, 14m N of Exeter

This attractive market town is dominated by one of the finest churches in Devon, **St Andrew's**. The splendour

Overleaf: Ilfracombe

of the late Perpendicular church reflects the prosperity of Cullompton's former wool industry, which flourished in the 16th-17th c. The building has a fine barrel roof and an impressive painted rood screen. The *Lane Aisle* (1526) with its fine fan vaulting was built as a personal memorial to a rich wool merchant. 17th-c. survivals in the town are *The Manor House Hotel* (1603, enlarged in the 18th c.) and the nearby *Walronds* (same date). The town has cider orchards in the neighbourhood and the oldest working paper mill in Devon (*Higher Kingsmill*, 1757). *Uffculme*, 5m NE, has an interesting working mill museum.

Dart Valley Railway
3C/4C & 4C

Buckfastleigh – Totnes, return via Staverton
Paignton – Kingswear.

The Buckfastleigh – Totnes line is one of the best-known steam-train routes in the country, with vintage locomotives pulling vintage carriages a distance of 7m along the old Great Western Railway track. For a supplementary charge passengers can travel first class in an observation car called the *Devon Belle*, giving splendid views of the Dart and the rolling countryside. At Buckfastleigh Station is a model railway exhibition, 7½ inch gauge steam railway, signal box and station shop, café and museum. (It is not possible to join the train at Totnes.)

There is a separate line (also 7m) from Paignton to Kingswear along the coast. From Kingswear a steamer can be taken up the River Dart to Totnes.

Dartington Hall
4C

Historic house and arts centre off A384, 2m NW of Totnes

Dartington Hall was built in 1388 by John Holland, Duke of Exeter, half-brother of King Richard II. After his execution for murder and a lapse of 70 years the estate passed to another family, but by the beginning of this century it was derelict. It was purchased in 1925 by Dorothy and Leonard Elmhirst, remarkable Anglo-American philanthropists who set up a pioneering educational, artistic and cultural centre

with the ideal of reviving the countryside through creative industry and education. The Amadeus String Quartet was formed here, and Henry Moore and the potter Bernard Leach both taught at the Arts Centre. There are now craft centres, a model farm, an art school, and regular festivals, short courses and concerts.

The **Hall** itself is undoubtedly the most spectacular medieval mansion in Devon, with a quadrangle little changed over the centuries and a great hall 40ft by 80ft with a (new) hammerbeam roof. The original *tiltyard*, built for jousts, may still be seen in the beautiful gardens, and in the grounds is a fine early Henry Moore sculpture. In the village at Shinner's Bridge, 1m SW, is *The Cider Press Centre*, which has interesting shops selling the top-quality local crafts, glass and pottery and the celebrated vegetarian restaurant *Cranks*. 200yds E of the village on the A385 is *Dartington Tweed Mill* which visitors can go round during factory hours. (The world-famous glass is made in *Great Torrington*).

Dartmoor
Central Devon

Dartmoor is a massive granite plateau created during volcanic activity millions of years ago and subsequently eroded. The National Park extends over 365 sq m and encompasses the barren moor of the centre and lush woodland gorges and fast streams around the edges (e.g. *Lydford* Gorge and *Becky Falls*). The moorland is characterised by peat bogs, grazing sheep and ponies (not wild but owned by Dartmoor Commoners), and the granite outcrops or tors such as *Haytor*, *Hound Tor* and Bowerman's Nose (see *Manaton*). Dartmoor has been inhabited for at least 3000 years and there are innumerable stone circles, hut circles, hill forts and burial tombs, amongst the best known of which are *Grimspound* and *Spinster's Rock*. From the 12th c. tin, silver, arsenic, copper and most recently china clay have been mined (see *Mary Tavy*) and the wealth and prosperity of the four ancient Stannary (or tin) Towns, (*Ashburton*, *Chagford*, *Lydford* and *Tavistock*) date from the late Middle Ages. The famous clapper bridges, built for the pack-horses carrying tin or wool, date from this period or later (see *Postbridge* and *Two Bridges*).

The bleak moorland is almost completely empty, and there are no roads across the N part. (*Cranmere Pool* at the centre is more than 8m from the nearest road.) This isolation makes Dartmoor very popular with walkers. However, it is also popular with the army, and large tracts are often closed for firing practice (when the red flags are flying). With its mists, peat bogs and remoteness, Dartmoor can be dangerous, and walkers should never set off unless properly equipped (compass, whistle, OS map, boots, protective clothing etc.) and without leaving details of their whereabouts. Three circular walks on Dartmoor are described (*Walks 6, 7 & 8*, p.26).

Around the periphery in the lush valleys are some of Britain's loveliest villages, among them *Buckland-in-the-Moor*, *Gidleigh*, *Lustleigh*, *Manaton* and *Widecombe-in-the-Moor*.

Visitors to Dartmoor can get advice and help on planning excursions and walks, dates of army manoeuvres and booklets from the *National Park Information Centres* which operate Apr-Oct; (near *Ashburton*, *Dunsford*, *Okehampton*, *Postbridge*, *Princetown* and *Tavistock*). The headquarters, just outside *Bovey Tracey* in a classical Georgian mansion, is open all year.

Dartmoor Wildlife Park   4B
Off A38 near Sparkwell, 8m NE of Plymouth

This 25-acre wildlife sanctuary has over 100 species from tigers and wolves to water fowl and guinea pigs in natural, well-landscaped enclosures.

Dartmouth   4C
Town on A379, 11m S of Torquay. Event: Royal Regatta (Aug Bank Hol). EC Wed MD Fri.
Inf: Tel (08043) 2282

Built on the steep wooded valley overlooking the River Dart, Dartmouth's importance has always been as a first-class defensive port. The Crusaders of 1147 and 1190 left for Jerusalem from here, and from the 13th c. the town was made rich by the wine trade with Bordeaux. From the 17th c., the town's trade with Newfoundland became its main source of prosperity, and most recently, as a plaque on the quay records, the United States 'D' Day Normandy force left from Dartmouth with 485 amphibious craft on June 3, 1944. Dartmouth is the home of the massive **Britannia Royal Naval Training College** (1905) where almost every naval officer, including King George VI, The Duke of Edinburgh, Prince Charles and Prince Andrew have been trained.

The 'station', which has no railway and no track, but which is used by the passenger ferry, is near the centre of the town. To the N, in Coronation Park (car park), is the **Newcomen Engine House**, containing the working 'atmospheric steam engine' of *c.* 1712. This pioneering invention by a Dartmouth native was the first effective use of steam power, and paved the way for the development of steam trains. W in Duke Street is **The Butterwalk** of 1635-40, with granite pillars, half-timbering and fine carved wooden figures. In addition to shops it houses the *Dartmouth Museum*, with its exhibition of model ships. At the top end of the street is the *Market Square*, laid out in 1812 and still used every Friday.

Crossing Fore Street to the S is Anzac Street, with its attractive houses and the eccentric *Henley Museum*, a local man's personal collection. At the end of Anzac Street is **St Saviour's Church**, consecrated in 1372 but largely rebuilt at a time of prosperity between 1614-1630. It has a fine painted screen of 1480, and an unusual Jacobean stone pulpit. Tucked away behind a curtain at the W end is the old town fire engine of 1734. On the S door are some 17th-c. ironwork leopards, grinning ferociously through their foliage.

Beyond the church in Higher Street are a number of good houses, the best of which is the half-timbered pub, *The*

Hope Cove

Dartmoor scene   *Opposite: Hartland Point*

Cherub (1380). It is worth observing that before the reclamation of the flat area of the town to the N of the church in the late 16th c., this part of Dartmouth was at the river's edge.

On the river at the S end of the town is **Bayard's Cove**, a lovely cobbled courtyard from whence *The Mayflower* set off on July 31, 1620 with another boat, *The Speedwell*, only to be forced to return to Plymouth when the latter ship sprang a leak. *Bayard's Cove Castle*, little more than a tower, was built in 1537 against the French.

1m S of the town is **Dartmouth Castle** and *St Petrock's Church*, the former built against the French in 1481 and incorporating the most advanced designs for cannon fire, and the latter dating from 1641. In times of danger in the Middle Ages, chains were stretched across the river from the castle to Kingswear castle on the opposite bank.

From Dartmouth there is a choice of three ferries to *Kingswear over the river, and numerous boat trips around the coast and up-river to *Totnes. The *Royal Devon Yacht Club* and *Dartmouth Sailing Club* are based in the town, and there are opportunities for diving.

Dawlish 3D
Town on A379, 13m S of Exeter. EC Thur.
Inf: Tel (0626) 863589

Until the 19th c. this was a small fishing village, but in 1803 *The Lawn* was laid down. It is a lovely park with pools and ornamental bridges over *Dawlish Water*, the stream that divides Dawlish down the middle. The town has many pretty villas including the delightful *Gothic Priory*, and remains a very sedate watering place. The poet John Keats stayed here with his brother at the beginning of the 19th c. in search of a cure for consumption, and Charles Dickens liked the town so much that he made it Nicholas Nickleby's birthplace. Brunel brought the railway through Dawlish right along the seashore, but far from ruining the town it adds special character, with its picturesque station. There is access to the sandy beaches (excellent swimming)

under the railway viaduct. A charming little *Museum* in Barton Terrace has a local history collection with bric-à-brac and Victorian dolls.

Dawlish Warren, 2m up the coast, is a camping and caravan site of little appeal, though it does contain the *South Devon Railway Museum and Model Railway* with interesting exhibits. The high sandstone cliffs have marvellous views and sustain rare flowers. 1m W is *Luscombe Castle* (not open) a fine 'Gothick' mansion of 1800.

Dittisham 4C
Village 4m NW of Dartmouth

A tiny hamlet in the most picturesque of surroundings on the banks of the Dart, and best seen from the river on the 10m cruise from Dartmouth to Totnes. The impressive **St George's Church** dates back to the 14th c. and has a fine 15th-c. pulpit. An offshore rock (*Anchor Stone*), seen at low tide, is said to have been a retreat of Sir Walter Raleigh when he wanted to smoke his pipe. The Elizabethan anti-smoking lobby was obviously powerful.

Doddiscombsleigh 3C
Village off B3193, 12m SW of Exeter

The 15th-c. **St Michael's Church** boasts the finest medieval glass in Devon, complete in five windows despite Victorian restoration. The remoteness of the village ensured the preservation of the church during the Civil War. Everybody is welcome at *The Nobody*, an excellent and ancient inn.

Drewsteignton 3C
Dartmoor village off A30, 13m W of Exeter

This delightful thatched village is perched above the River Teign. It has a fine 16th-c. granite *church*, but the main interest of the parish is not in the village. 1m SE is **Fingle Bridge**, a three-arch 16th-c. bridge spanning the Teign on the lushest fringe of Dartmoor. One of the loveliest spots in Devon, it is a perfect picnic spot. 1m SW is *Castle Drogo* (NT) a truly remarkable granite castle built this century. 2m W is *Spinster's Rock*, a prehistoric burial

The Harbour, Torquay

Cruise boat on the River Dart, Totnes   Below: Woolacombe Bay

place and the only one to be found in the Dartmoor area. There is a 4m circular walk, starting at Fingle Bridge and going up the Teign Gorge past Castle Drogo. (See *Walk* 7, p.26.)

Dunsford 3C
Dartmoor village and Nature Reserve off B3212, 10m SW of Exeter. Nat Park Inf Centre: Tel (0647) 52018

The village is set in a thickly wooded valley and has a church with many monuments to the Fulford family, who have lived in the same house, *Great Fulford* (Tudor, enlarged 1780) since 1084 (not open). 1m W on the B3212 is *Dunsford Wood Nature Reserve*, 4m of delightful woodland country noted for its fine display of spring flowers.

East Budleigh
See *Budleigh Salterton*

Eggesford 2B
Village on A377, 13m NW of Crediton

A convenient base for two nature trails, each 1m long, through *Eggesford Forest* (open throughout the year and starting from the picnic area on A377 2m S of the station). *Eggesford House*, 1m W of the station, rebuilt in 1830 with turrets and battlements, was dismantled in 1917 and is now a sad ruin being swallowed up by the forest.

2m W is the *Ashley Countryside Collection*, showing farm and farmhouse equipment including a remarkable display of 45 different kinds of sheep.

Ermington 4B
Village on B3210, 1m off A379, 11m E of Plymouth

A delightful village with a 13-14th-c. *Church* famous for its twisted spire. Inside is a fine 17th-c. screen and Elizabethan monuments.

1m S on the other side of the A379 is **Flete**, a rambling granite mansion built in 1878 by Norman Shaw for the millionaire banker H.B. Mildmay. Masked by Shaw's building is the original small Jacobean house. The mansion is now divided into flats, but the main reception rooms are open to the public. The gardens are beautifully kept.

EXETER 3C

*building, etc. of outstanding interest

Population 97,000

Tourist Information Civic Centre. Tel Exeter (0392) 72434. Mon-Sat 9-5.30

EC Wed, Sat   **MD** Mon, Fri

Places of interest
All places listed are open to the public and described in the text that follows

Churches

*****Exeter Cathedral**
7.30am – after Choral Evensong (5.30, 3pm Fri)

St Martin Cathedral Close

St Mary Arches Mary Arches Street

St Mary Steps West Street

*****St Nicholas Priory** Mint Street

St Olave Fore Street

*****St Pancras** Guildhall Shopping Centre

Historic Buildings

*****Guildhall** High Street
Mon-Sat 10-5.30

Ancient Sites

Underground Passages Princesshay
Tue-Sat 2-5

Museums

Devonshire Regiment Museum Barrack Road
Mon-Fri (not Bank Hol) 9.30-12.30 & 1.30-4.15

*****Maritime Museum** The Quay
Daily 10-5

Rougemont House Museum Castle Street
Tue-Sat 10-1 & 2-5.15

Royal Albert Museum & Art Gallery Queen Street
Tue-Sat 10-5.15

Historic Inns
See p.23

Old Exeter with Church of St Mary Steps

The county town of Devon, Exeter has a long history as a prosperous regional centre. First a prehistoric settlement, it was an important garrison town in Roman times and the grid-like central crossing (or Carfax) of North Street, South Street, Fore Street and High Street dates from that time. The city walls built by the Romans and repaired in the 10th c. gave protection against the Danes and were the crucial factor in deciding the clergy to move their cathedral from Crediton to Exeter in 1050. One of the last towns to hold out against William the Conqueror, Exeter was finally defeated in 1068, after which a castle was built to keep the town in order. A prosperous town and busy port, Exeter had the first ship canal in the country, built in Elizabethan times, and was a major serge exporter in Stuart times. The medieval city within the walls survived almost intact until May 5, 1942 when German bombs destroyed most, though not all of the old buildings. Recent building has however been quite sensitive (particularly by the river) and despite the losses Exeter remains an attractive and interesting place to visit.

Exeter Cathedral

Exeter Cathedral Near the centre of the Roman city, there has been a church on this site for 1300 years. In 1050 Leofric was enthroned as the first bishop of the see of Exeter, which at that time covered both Devon and Cornwall. Nothing remains of the early churches or Bishop Leofric's Saxon building, but the great *transeptal towers*, 150ft high, survive the Norman cathedral (1133) and have rows of blind arches with the characteristic Norman zig-zag patterns. This is a unique position for cathedral towers and explains both the unusual appearance of the cathedral and the length of the roof vault. The body of the church (excluding the Lady Chapel) is almost entirely the work of one man, John Grandisson, Bishop from 1327-1369, who proudly wrote to Pope John

XXII that 'the cathedral in Exeter is marvellous in beauty and when completed will surpass every church in England and France'. Exeter is rare among English cathedrals for its harmonious unity, and miraculous in surviving (after one direct hit) the bombing that flattened the rest of medieval Exeter in 1942.

The *W front* is decorated with a three-tier image screen and a large window (modern glass) above. The 14th-c. sculptures, representing angels, prophets, kings and soldiers are in process of restoration. Inside, the view down the *nave* is incomparable: Exeter has the longest unbroken Gothic vaulting in the world (more than 300ft). The *rib vaulting* is characterised by bold bosses, each one different and brightly

Cathedral Close, Exeter

painted. High up in the fifth bay on the N side is the 14th-c. *minstrels' gallery* with cheerful angels playing a variety of instruments including cymbals, bagpipes and trumpets. It is still used for carol concerts. At the E end of the nave is the elaborate carved *choir screen* of Purbeck marble (early 14th-c.), containing two altars. In medieval times the screen marked the limit for townspeople: only priests were allowed into the sanctuary beyond. Above the screen is the huge organ of 1665.

In the *N transept* is a fascinating late 15th-c. *clock* which shows the earth at the centre of the dial (and of the universe) with the moon and sun revolving round it indicating the hours and the phases of the moon. The works (16th-17th-c.) have been removed from the clock, which is now operated by electricity. Above is one of the heaviest bells in the country – the Great Peter – weighing 125 cwt. The 14 bells of the *S transept* tower make up the second heaviest peal in the country (after Liverpool). Proceeding along the *N choir aisle*, the *Choir* is entered. Its most spectacular feature is the *E window* with 14th-c. glass, and the remarkable oak *Bishop's Throne* of 1313, with an ornately carved canopy 59ft high. The choir stalls are modern but the *misericords* are medieval and exquisitely carved with animals. The misericords were only meant as perches and not seats for the weary choristers and they are said to be so finely hinged that if one fell asleep, the misericords fell forwards with a resounding thud!

Returning to the *N choir aisle*, at the E end is *Sir John Speke's Chantry* (1517), the finest of a number of medieval and Tudor *chantry chapels* to past bishops and Earls of Devon. Since the chantries were built as an act of devotion to reduce their founder's time in purgatory, they are all exquisitely carved and highly coloured. At the E end of the cathedral is the *Lady Chapel*, containing a very rare Saxon slab tomb, possibly to Bishop Leofric, builder of the Saxon church. At the E end of the S choir aisle is *Bishop Oldham's Chantry*, commemorating the founder of Manchester Grammar School.

The *Chapter House* beyond the S transept is 12th and 15th-c. and has some controversial modern sculptures.

The **Cathedral Close** is one of the largest in the country. To the SE of the cathedral is the *Bishop's Palace*, where the library containing medieval manuscripts may be viewed (weekdays 2-5). Nos 9-11 *Cathedral Close* are fine medieval houses, built of the local red sandstone (unlike the cathedral, built of the better but much more expensive Beer stone). Nos 6-8 are also medieval but were refaced in Georgian times. Mol's Coffee House, almost on the corner, was a favourite meeting place for Sir Francis Drake, Hawkins and Frobisher, the great Elizabethan sea captains, as was *The Ship Inn* in the nearby Martin's Lane. Opposite *Mol's*, the *Royal Clarence Hotel* (1768) is said to be the first building in the country to have been called a 'hotel'.

On the corner of the Close and Catherine Street is *St Martin's Church*, one of Exeter's lovely little medieval churches. Originally there were 28 chapels within the city walls, but only five stand today. Consecrated in 1065, St Martin's is a 15th-c. building with 17th- and 18th-c. furnishings. Just beyond it, in Catherine Street, are the ruins of *St Catherine's Almhouses and Chapel*, which from 1450 until 1942 provided relief to 13 poor men of the city.

At the end of Catherine Street is Bedford Street and at its E end is *Southernhay*. By 1600 the old city within the walls was completely full and expansion was only possible outside. Southernhay, an 18th-c. avenue of terraced houses, was one of the first new developments and would be a credit to Cheltenham or Bath.

At the N end of Southernhay is *Princesshay*, a pedestrian precinct in the middle of which is the entrance to the remarkable **Underground Passages**, the cool dark tunnels which are the remains of the city's medieval water supply (open to the public). From here, crossing the High Street by turning left and right, enter *Castle Street*. At the far end is the gatehouse of **Rougemont Castle**. This is all that remains of William the Conqueror's fortress, for on its site are the *Court Buildings* (1774). Just in front of the Gatehouse on the left is *Rougemont House Museum*, built in 1769 and now a museum of local archeology and history. Going through Rougemont Gardens and the city wall at *Athelstan's Tower* (1200) you reach *Northernhay*, England's oldest public park, laid out in 1612. At the W end of the park is Queen Street. Returning towards the High Street, the **Royal Albert Museum** is on the left. Housed in an ostentatious Victorian building, it has collections of paintings, costumes, natural history and a Red Indian shrunken head.

A little further down, on the other side of the street, is the *Guildhall Shopping Centre*, entered through the Doric colonnade of the old Civic Hall (1838). At its heart is the *Church of St Pancras*. This tiny church (with only a small chancel and nave) dates from 1191, though much of the stonework is 13th-c.

Return through the precinct to the *High Street* where there are a number of old houses and shop-fronts. Of greatest interest is the **Guildhall** (to the right). Its granite-pillared façade is Tudor but inside, the hall itself dates from 1330 (roof 1470), and the site has been in continuous use as a Council building since 1190, making it the oldest municipal building in Britain. 60yds beyond it, but very easily missed, is

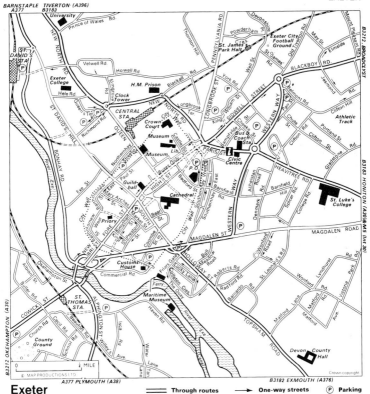

Exeter

════ Through routes   ⟶ One-way streets   Ⓟ Parking

Parliament Street. Not for large eaters, it is the narrowest steet in the world: only 25in wide at its thinnest part and with no passing places.

Crossing the Carfax (Roman intersection of the town's main streets) into Fore Street, you reach Mary Arches Street on the right, in which is the 12th-c. *Church* of that name. A little further down Fore Street, also on the right, is the interesting *St Olave's Church* with the tower built inside the body of the church. Like so many of Exeter's medieval buildings it was very cramped for space and when it was enlarged in the 14th c. it filled the only available space which explains its unusual 'L' shape.

In Mint Street further down is **St**

Nicholas Priory (15th c.), the last surviving complete monastic guesthouse in the country. It has a spectacular 11th-c. cellar and is now run by the Exeter Museums Service. Continuing downhill, go left along King Street and turn right into *Stepcote Hill*, the medieval entrance to the city. At the bottom are some fine medieval houses, including the *House That Moved* (about 75yds in 1964 to save it from demolition). The *Church of St Mary Steps* has a glorious 16th-c. clock with three villainous-looking figures to strike the hours.

Half-right, by the River Exe and between the two new bridges are the recently excavated and restored remains of Exeter's **medieval bridge**. Once

600ft long, seven arches remain and the foundations of *St Edmund's Church* which once stood at the E end. It would once have been covered with shops and houses and is an impressive reminder of an important medieval city.

From the bridge (going through the subway) it is possible to walk downstream along the river to the 17th-c. *Customs House*, Exeter's first brick building. On the quay further along is the **Exeter Maritime Museum**, which has over 100 boats from all over the world on display including coracles, a sampan and a gondola. The adjacent *Prospect Inn* is a delightful place to watch the world go by with a pint. From here it is a short walk back up the hill to the cathedral. From the Maritime Museum there is an interesting canal-side walk to *Topsham. (See *Walk 11*, p.26.)

1½m from the cathedral, in their barracks on the Topsham Road, is the **Devonshire Regiment Museum** which displays their distinguished military record.

Exmoor
NE Devon/Somerset border

The Exmoor National Park, covering 265 sq m, lies mainly in Somerset. Of the variety of landscape within its boundary – moorland, heathland and coastal – Devon has the best example of the latter, seen from windswept walks on the Somerset and North Devon Coast Path or from the steep dramatic roads to the W of Lynton. Although not so rich in prehistoric sites as Dartmoor, there is scattered evidence of Bronze and Iron Age settlement, most notably at *Chapman Barrows*, SE of Parra-combe. The moorland is rich grazing country, supporting sheep, ponies, red deer and grouse. Once a royal forest, sacred to hunting monarchs, much of Exmoor's woodland has now gone and agriculture has taken its place. The area is still very beautiful, however, and offers excellent walking and riding. See also *Combe Martin*, *Countisbury*, *Lynmouth and Lynton*, *Molland* and *Parracombe*. (See also *Walk 9*, p.26.)

Exmoor Bird Gardens
1B
Off B3226 at South Stowford (N of Bratton Fleming), 9m NE of Barnstaple

A landscaped open-air aviary containing tropical birds, penguins and rare breeds of poultry. There is also a pets' corner.

Exmouth
3D
Pop: 26,840 11m S of Exeter (A376). EC Wed
Inf: Tel (03952) 3744

Burnt by the Danes and an important port under Edward III, Exmouth became well-known in the late 18th c. for its 'high rank among watering places of the county'. It received a boost in the early 19th c. when two famous widows, Lady Nelson and Lady Byron, came to live in the lovely Georgian street of *The Beacon* at No 6 and No 19 respectively. The old centre has recently been redeveloped and some Victorian buildings have been lost, but much remains, including the *High Street*, *Tower Street* and *Albion Street* which has more than a dozen antique and junk shops. *The Esplanade* of grand Victorian terraces has a charming old-world atmosphere and at its E end is *The Maer*, a grassy park with all the usual attractions of an English seaside resort but including the world's largest 00 gauge model railway complex (180ft scenic layout). From the front there are marvellous views towards Torbay.

There is an interesting small harbour and dock area, hidden from the rest of the town at the W end of the Esplanade. From it pleasure trips can be taken up the coast to Torquay and Lyme Regis or up-river to Exeter, and a ferry plies across the Exe to *Starcross*.

2m E of the town is the **Sandy Bay Steam and Countryside Museum** with agricultural machinery, thatched cottages, working steam engines, and a paddock with Shire horses, ponies and farmyard pets.

2m N, just off the A376 in Summer Lane is **A La Ronde**, a 16-sided Gothic folly built in 1798 by two eccentric spinsters. This fantasy house has an octagonal hall 60ft high, encrusted with shells and adorned with imitation birds made of feathers. Shells also feature in the decor of the drawing room and the house boasts a very early flushing lavatory. A little further up Summer Lane, *Point of View* is a chapel and almshouses built by the same two spinsters to assist four poor old maids.

Farway Countryside Park   2D
Off B3174, 5m NW of Seaton

130 acres of nature trails, deer parks, rare farmyard animals, pony rides, donkey cart trips and grass skiing. 1m S is the Iron Age *Blackbury Castle.

Fernworthy Reservoir   3B
Off B3212, 5m W of Moretonhampstead

Although man-made to supply water to the Torbay area, the lake is well stocked with trout, and a permit to fish can be obtained from the house at the head of the lake. The wooded landscape is noted for its many stone circles and barrows and numerous mining relics, including the ruins of the old blowing house near the shore of the reservoir.

Filleigh   1B
Village on A361, 3m NW of South Molton

A lovely village centred on the estate of the Fortesque family whose seat, *Castle Hill* (open by appointment only) is ½m NE of the village church. The mansion, built in 1684 and subsequently enlarged (1730s and 1840s) was finally rebuilt in 1935 in the original style. It is set in a vast park landscaped by William Kent. The *Church* has also had its rebuildings but retains two interesting brasses to the Fortesque family dated 1570.

Fingle Bridge
See *Drewsteignton*

Flete
See *Ermington*

Frithelstock   2A
Village between A386 and A388, 1½m W of Great Torrington

Notable for the ruins of an *Augustinian Priory* founded *c.* 1220, of which the W end still stands, and the adjacent *Church* with its lofty tapering tower, barrel roof, delightful bench ends and royal arms in plaster of 1677.

Gidleigh   3B
Dartmoor village off A382, 7m NW of Moretonhampstead

The parish is a large one of open moor (common grazing land) and farmland. At the bottom of the parish runs the River Teign and one of its tributaries the most beautiful oak woodland. The village itself is minute. There is little more than two cottages, a youth hostel (which is also the village post office), a ruined Norman castle keep and the parish church. Mainly 14th-c., **Holy Trinity Church** has a fine screen of 1530, and propped up against the outside walls are unusual 17th-c. painted gravestones. The churchyard has a small stream running through it, and is renowned as a 'natural nature reserve' for small mammals and birds, including breeding owls.

Gnome Reserve   2A
Off A388 at West Putford, 10m N of Holsworthy

More than 600 gnomes living happily in a wood with a stream running through. Probably the most unnerving sight in the West Country, but undoubtedly unique.

Grand Western Canal   2D
Tiverton (A373) to Burrow Farm, N of A38

The canal, cut in 1810, was designed for transporting coal and limestone. However in 1844 it was superseded by the arrival of the Great Western Railway at Tiverton. An 11½m stretch, starting from *Tiverton*, is still navigable. There is a good path along the length of the canal, and a car park and café at the Tiverton basin. There are horse-drawn long-boat trips from Tiverton during the summer (see p.21), and a circular walk incorporating the canal towpath from Tiverton (See *Walk 12*, p.27).

Great Torrington   2B
Town on A386, 5m S of Bideford. EC Wed MD alternate Mon. Inf: Tel (08052) 3169

The town, set in lovely countryside, enjoys a wonderful position perched steeply over a bend in the River Torridge. Great Torrington has been a borough since the 12th c., and was heavily fought over during the Civil

War. The *Market Square* around which it is built would do credit to a town ten times its size. In the square is the *Town Hall*, rebuilt 1861, which houses the *Torrington Museum*. Off the NW corner is **St Michael's Church**, with its distinctive tower and spire. The latter was built in 1830: outside the entrance an inscription records the destruction of the original 14th-c. church. This occurred in the Civil War, when the church and over 200 Royalist prisoners inside were blown up by 80 barrels of gunpowder, stored in the church during its use by Oliver Cromwell's men as an arsenal (the church was rebuilt in 1651).

Great Torrington has many attractive houses of different periods. Opposite the churchyard is the 18th-c. *Palmer House*, where Sir Joshua Reynolds and Dr Johnson stayed. S of the Market Square, in South Street, look through the window of *No 28* (c. 1700). The ceiling here, with a centrepiece of musical instruments, is exceptional in Devon.

From the adjacent car park, steps lead down to a splendid short walk E along the path overlooking the river and a splendid bowl of rural Devon landscape. Here are the remains of a 13th-c. *castle*, partially restored. **Dartington Glass** (School Lane, near the church) moved to Torrington in 1967, bringing with it Scandinavian master-craftsmen. Conducted tours of the factory are offered from 9.30-10.30 and 12-3.30. 1m SE are the charming *Rosemoor Gardens*, while 2m S, S of the tiny sister village of *Little Torrington*, is the excellent *Gribble Inn*.

Grimspound   3C
Ancient site. 2m S of B3212, 7m SW of Moretonhampstead

Once a highly important fortified Bronze Age village, this site, which covers 4 acres, is surrounded by a circular wall of rough granite blocks. Inside are 24 hut circles (one partially restored), most of which were lived in; the remainder used for animals and storehouses. ½m S is *Hameldown Tor* (1736ft), highest peak in E Dartmoor.

Hallsands   4C
Ruined village on S coast off A379, 12m SE of Kingsbridge

A ghost village reached by path from Torcross (3m). Hallsands was destroyed by a violent gale in 1917, leaving half-demolished houses – now picturesque ruins. An ideal place for a picnic. 2m S is *Start Point*.

Hartland   1A
Small town off A39, 14m W of Bideford

In the midst of bleak and thinly-populated farming country in the extreme W of the county, Hartland is the gateway to splendid coastal scenery. The little town has some attractive houses, and is served by the *Chapel of St John* (1839), built on the site of the old Town Hall and incorporating its clock of 1622. 1½m W is *Hartland Abbey*, founded as a college for 'secular canons' in the 11th c. but made into a grand private mansion with additions from Tudor times onwards (not open). ½m further W is the **Church of St Nectan**, one of the glories of N Devon. Dating from 1350, it replaces a building erected by King Harold's mother, Gytha, as a landmark for ships (which explains why it is so far from the town). Its 15th-c. tower is one of the highest in Devon (128ft) with many buttresses. Inside, the church has a fine barrel roof with painted panels above the centre of the nave. The magnificent 15th-c. rood screen – the largest in Devon – is exquisitely carved and retains much of its original colouring. The font is late Norman, c. 1170. On the left side of the chancel is a 14th-c. altar tomb from Hartland Abbey, carved from Cornish stone.

1m further W is **Hartland Quay**, once a busy port, which has seen no shipping since the destruction of the man-made harbour last century in a storm. This wild jagged stretch of Atlantic coast is notorious to shipping. As the old saying goes:

> From Hartland Point
> To Padstow Light
> A watery Grave by
> Day or Night

Hartland Quay Museum records the shipwrecks as well as the natural history of the coast. There is exhilarating cliff-top walking, 5m S to the Cornish border, taking in the 70ft waterfall at *Speke's Mill Mouth*, which can also be reached by a circular walk of 6m. (See *Walk 5*, p.25.)

3m N is **Hartland Point** (also accessible by road from Hartland) a magnificent headland 325ft high, with a *lighthouse* of 1874 at its foot (open to public in summer in good weather).

Haytor   3C
Natural rock outcrop off A382, 4m W of Bovey Tracey, 8m NW of Newton Abbot

With a large car park near its foot, Haytor is the most visited of the tors, and an easy climb rewarded by magnificent views. 1m E is the shell of a huge hotel, destroyed by fire many years ago but picturesque in its desolation. To the N are the scars of the disused quarries that furnished the stone for the British Museum and many other London buildings, and the granite rails of an early railway used for transporting the stone. 1½m NW is *★Hound Tor* and 4m N are the renowned *★Becky Falls*.

Hele   1B
Village on N coast (A399), 1½m E of Ilfracombe

Apart from the fine beach at Hele Bay, Hele has an interesting relic: a 16th-c. *watermill*, authentically restored, with an 18ft overshot water wheel. Whole-meal flour is still made on the premises.

Hembury Fort
See *Honiton*

Holsworthy   2A
Small town on A388 and A3072, 20m NW of Okehampton. Event: St Peter's Fair (Jul). EC Tue MD Wed.

The viaduct by which the railway came and went is an impressive monument to Victorian railway-mania. The town is now 'off the track', except on market day when it springs to life. Visitors are catered for by the ancient *White Hart* in Fore Street.

5m NE at Thornbury is the *Devon*

Museum of Mechanical Music, with musical boxes, fairground organs and a variety of other fascinating instruments.

Honiton   2D & 4D
Town on A30, 17m NE of Exeter. Events: Annual Fair (3rd week in Jul) Carnival (last week in Oct). EC Thur MD Tue & Sat

Thanks to the by-pass, Honiton is almost completely unspoiled. Its **High Street** (Roman in origin) is long and wide, with dozens of lovely Georgian two-storey houses built after disastrous fires in 1747 and 1765. The best building of the pre-fire period is *Marwood House* (1619) at the E end, and the thatched cottages (some 16th-c.) of *St Margaret's Hospital* at the W end.

Once very prosperous, Honiton is now best known for its lace. Huguenot lacemakers settled here in Elizabethan times, and examples of lace from all periods are on display at the *All Hallows Museum*, housed in the 16th-c. chapel of the *Grammar School* (1770). The famous *Honiton Pottery* in the High Street is open to the public, and should not be missed.

For those with a taste for the eccentric, the Victorian *Tower* on Honiton Hill is worth a look, as is *Copper Castle* on the Axminster Road, a delightful castellated toll-house. 3m NW on the A373 (lay-by) is **Hembury Fort**, a massive Stone Age camp 1085ft long and 330ft wide, occupied for 4000 years up to Roman times. One of the most magnificent views in the county is from the fort to the SW, across Exeter to Dartmoor.

Hope Cove   4B
Village on S coast off A381, 6m SW of Kingsbridge

There are two parts to Hope: the Outer which is modern and Inner Hope which is ancient and consists of little more than a shop and handful of thatched cottages. It was once a noted smuggling centre and crabbing harbour. The fine rocky sea-shore and cliffs are a minute's walk from the car park, and the coastal path to *Bolt Head* via *Bolt Tail* (6m, see *★Salcombe*) takes in some of Britain's wildest and most exciting coastal scenery. 2m N is *Thurlestone, with its first-class golf course, while between the two villages are many secluded beaches.

Hound Tor 3C
Off B3344, 2m SW of Manaton, 15m NW of Newton Abbot

A granite outcrop shaped like a dog's face, with outstanding views to the NW, best known for the legend surrounding *Jay's Grave* nearby. A young girl named Kitty Jay hanged herself in the 19th c. and was buried by the roadside near Hound Tor. From that day to this fresh flowers have been placed regularly on the grave, no one knows by whom, and watchers have had some eerie moments (without solving the mystery). 1½m SE is *Haytor and 2m NE on the B3344 are the beautiful *Becky Falls.

Ilfracombe 1B
Town on N coast (A399/A361), 13m N of Barnstaple. EC Thur MD Sat. Inf: Tel (0271) 63001

North Devon's leading resort, a friendly town with numerous entertainments, well located for excursions to Exmoor.

A seaport in medieval times, Ilfracombe was little more than a fishing village when the railway arrived in 1874. Its bracing climate, and attractive harbour and coastline, appealed greatly to the Victorians, who created a resort which still reflects a robust and extravagant age. The town is rich in public gardens, cleverly landscaped over the steep contours, and fanciful buildings, such as the Pavilion theatre, which impressed visitors with their splendour.

The old part of the town is found in the harbour area: a long quay with fishermen's houses ranged along it is set on the N side of a small cove, guarding an inner harbour which makes a perfect refuge for the pleasure craft and fishing vessels. On top of *Lantern Hill* (100ft) at the mouth of the harbour, is the sailor's *St Nicholas Chapel*, originally 14th-c., a picturesque landmark and lighthouse. This is one of three excellent vantage points for viewing Ilfracombe's unique townscape: the others are *Capstone Hill* to the W (156ft) with zig-zag paths to the summit, and *Hillsborough Hill* (447ft) to the E. From Hillsborough, the site of Ilfracombe's first prehistoric settlement, there are views reaching for many miles.

Ilfracombe has a number of secluded coves and beaches offering safe bathing. The best are *Rapparee* Cove to the W of Hillsborough opposite the harbour; *Hele Bay* to the E of Hillsborough, and – on the W side of Ilfracombe – the popular *Tunnel Beaches*. These are entered by tunnels in the cliff, approached from Northfield Road (small charge).

Many of Ilfracombe's varied gardens and entertainments can be found along the Sea Front (Wilder Road). There is a variety theatre (*Pavilion*), *museum*, mini golf-course and flower garden: the latter (*Jubilee Gardens*) particularly attractive at night with its coloured illuminations. There are many pleasant walks from Ilfracombe into the surrounding countryside. To the E, a cliff path around Hillsborough Hill leads to *Hele Bay: from the village of Hele the return to Ilfracombe can be made via *Chambercombe Manor. To the W of Ilfracombe the obvious choice is the route to *Lee via Torrs Walks and the South West Coast Path (3m). This walk can be continued (another 3m) to *Mortehoe and Morte Point; the return (from *Woolacombe) can be made by bus. (See also *Walk 4*, p.25.)

SW of Ilfracombe is *Bicclescombe Park* with its Tropical Wildlife Garden. Animals include monkeys, ocelots, flamingoes and parrots. There are also ponds and waterfalls, a Children's Boating Pool and restored *watermill* in working order.

Instow 1B
Village on A39, 3m N of Bideford

Despite its small size, Instow has its own quay, dating from 1620, and is the headquarters of the North Devon Yacht Club. There are fine sands, and a passenger ferry to *Appledore. The 13th-c. *Church* is in the old village up on the hill above the estuary and contains some interesting monuments. 1m S is the historic house and gardens of *Tapeley Park*.

Killerton House & Gardens (NT) 2D
Historic house off B3185 nr junction with B3181, 6m NE of Exeter

A classical 18th-c. house built by the Acland family and given to the National Trust by Sir Richard Acland in 1944. It contains family possessions, and a fine collection of period costumes. The gardens, laid out by John Veitch in the late 18th and early 19th c., are rich in exotic and native trees and plants. In the grounds is the quaint *chapel*, designed by C.R. Cockerell in the Norman style on the lines of the chapel of St Joseph of Arimathea at Glastonbury. The building of the chapel was held up by a swallow which had built a nest in the partly completed building: two carved nests on either side of one of the windows commemorate this. Above the house in the park is *Dolbury*, an Iron Age fort with commanding views.

Kilmington 4D
Village on A35, 2m W of Axminster

2m W of the village is the Baptist **Loughwood Meeting House**, built in 1653 and one of the oldest in the country. Outside it is very simple, and inside are the original box pews, gallery and barrel ceiling. Beneath the floorboards is the old baptistry, used for total immersion.

2m SW of the village is *Shute Barton*, a lovely 13th-c. manor house with 15th and 16th-c. additions. *Shute House*, a Georgian residence (now a school), 1/2m E was built in the 18th c. when the owners decided that the medieval house was not grand enough for them. (Neither are open.)

Kingsbridge 4C
Small town at intersection of A381 & A379, 21m SE of Plymouth. Event: Three-day fair, (3rd week in Jul). EC Thur MD Wed. Inf: Tel (0548) 3195

The spine of Kingsbridge is *Fore Street*, running uphill from the quay to the very limits of the town, and most of the best buildings are here, including the *Town Hall* and the *Shambles*, a covered arcade supported by granite pillars built in 1585 and refaced in 1796. Behind it is *St Edmund's Church* which dates back to the 13th c. On the S door of the Lady Chapel is this famous epitaph:

> Here lie I at the Chancel Door,
> Here lie I because I'm poor,
> The further in the more you'll pay,
> Here lie I as warm as they.

The 1670 *Grammar School* has been turned into the **Cookworthy Museum**, which besides items of local interest shows exhibits illustrating the development of the china clay industry. (William Cookworthy, a local man, was the discoverer of china clay in England.) There is a charming quay for small boats, with a neat promenade, along which runs a *Miniature Railway* for 1/2m. Kingsbridge is the market town and 'capital' of the area of Devon known as the South Hams, and regular auction sales are held in the capacious Market Hall.

Kingswear 4C
Village on B3205, 9m S of Torquay, ferry across estuary from Dartmouth

On the estuary opposite Dartmouth, Kingswear affords splendid views of the Dart, and the recent marina has brought a new interest to the place. *The Royal Dart Hotel* on the waterfront was built about 1850 in the fashionable Italian style, and has a lot of charm. *Kingswear Castle*, 1/2m SE, was built at the same time as Dartmouth Castle, c. 1490, but is much restored and not open to the public. In times of peril chains were linked between the two castles to keep out unwelcome vessels. One section of the *Dart Valley Railway* runs from Kingswear to Paignton.

Knightshayes Court (NT) 2D
Historic house off A396, 2m N of Tiverton

Designed 1868-74 by the eccentric William Burges, best known for his Cardiff Castle, this imposing sandstone mansion, with gables and jutting windows represents the Victorian dream of Gothic splendour. The interior is very Victorian, with colourful designs by

Burges and the decorating firm of Crace and Co. The billiard room has been converted into a restaurant.

Built for Sir John Heathcoat-Amory MP, grandson of the lace mill pioneer John Heathcoat, the house was bequeathed by *his* grandson to the National Trust in 1973. It was the last owner who was largely responsible for the delightful gardens, a mixture of formal and free, which are the most popular feature for visitors.

Lamerton
3A
Village off A384, 3m NW of Tavistock

This attractive village is at the NW end of the great arsenic and copper mining area of the mid-19th c. At that time the *Devon Great Consols* was one of the largest mines in the world, shipping 1200 tons of ore a day via *Morwellham Quay*. Other smaller mines with names such as the Huel Friendship, Tamar Silver-Lead Mine and Cad Quarries scattered the area. The old church burnt down in the last century, so the existing building is Victorian, but contains some fine tombs. The 16th-c. *Blacksmith's Arms* is worth visiting.

Lee
1B
Village on N coast off B3231, 3m W of Ilfracombe

An hour's walk from Ilfracombe through spectacular National Trust land, Lee is a picturesque seaside village at the head of a combe with a romantic aura of smuggling days. Lee has some pretty cottages, including *The Smugglers* on the beach dated 1627 and *The Old Maids' Cottage*, built in 1653. There is a well-signposted coastal path from Lee to *Morte Point* (5m) via *Bull Point*, taking in glorious combes, streams and beaches.

Lee Bay
1C
On N coast 1½m W of Lynton

Just to the W of the Valley of the Rocks, (see *Lynmouth and Lynton*) this well-conserved natural area includes a wooded valley, stream and two cliff-girt beaches with rock pools. A nature trail through the Lee Abbey Estate takes in most of the features (leaflets available).

The estate is entered through toll-gates: the walk starts at the car park by the lower toll and follows a route by footpath to the bay and then inland through woodland to *Lee Abbey*. This former medieval manor, rebuilt in the 19th c., is now the home of a Christian community and not open to the public.

Lewtrenchard
3A
Village off A30, 9m N of Tavistock

Lew House, now a hotel, and dated 1620 on the porch, was once the home of the well-known Victorian writer, the Rev S. Baring-Gould, author of books on the occult, on local history, and the hymn *Onward Christian Soldiers*. The house is alleged to be haunted by an ancestor of his who died in 1795. The delightfully situated **St Peter's Church** (15th-c.) is rich in memorials to the Baring-Gould family, and has a marvellous atmosphere of peace and tranquillity. It contains an elaborate screen, a large beautifully preserved painting near the altar, good bench ends and an enchanting small brass.

Lundy Island (NT)
20m off N coast, ferry from Ilfracombe

3m long and ½m wide, Lundy lies in the middle of the Bristol Channel, 1½hrs by boat from the mainland. In the Norse language, 'Lund-ey' means 'puffin isle' and is the traditional home of this bird (featured on the island's stamps).

The windswept island, with 400ft cliffs on the W, a central moorland plateau and a pleasantly vegetated E coast, is also a retreat for seals, wild goats and ponies, and – in addition to the puffin – countless other sea-birds, such as fulmars, kittiwakes and peregrines.

Lundy Island has had a chequered history. In the Middle Ages it was the haunt of pirates, who used it to prey on vessels bound for Bristol and other ports. In 1625 it was occupied by the Turks (for 14 days), then the Spaniards. In the reign of William and Mary, a party of Frenchmen invaded by anchoring a ship offshore under the pretext of wanting to bury their captain who had died at sea. With the permission of the islanders, they brought an unusually heavy coffin ashore, but once on land ripped it open to reveal guns and swords. They then proceeded to throw all the islanders' sheep in the sea, and plundered everything of value in the island before sailing away.

In 1747 Thomas Benson, MP for Barnstaple, leased Lundy and used it for nefarious enterprises. The boldest scheme was to divert convicts bound for penal colonies in America to the island and employ them as slave labour in the island's granite quarries (stone from Lundy was used for the Thames Embankment). After the exposure of another deceit (the insuring of a ship which he subsequently scuttled) Benson was forced to flee the country.

Among the island's man-made sights is a ruined 13th-c. castle, a disused lighthouse built in 1819 and replaced 1897, two churches and a manor house. There is a surprising amount to see in an area no greater than a large public park. A small community inhabits a village on the SE coast near the landing stage, and the inn is always conveniently open when the boat comes in. The island was purchased by the National Trust in 1969.

Lustleigh   3C
Dartmoor village off A382, 9m NW of Newton Abbot

One of the prettiest villages in Devon, reached only by tortuous lanes. The rose-covered thatched cottages nestle round a village green, while a stream passes through into the surrounding woodland. The 13th-c. *St John's Church* contains an interesting Norman font, fine effigies and a beautiful carved screen, and *The Cleave Inn* is noted for its excellent cuisine. In the summer there is an exhibition of paintings by local artists. There are magnificent walks through the woods surrounding Lustleigh, and *Lustleigh Cleave* is a spectacular wooded gorge. Nearby is *Becky Falls.

Lydford   3B
Small town off A386, 8m N of Tavistock.

In Saxon times Lydford was one of the most important towns in Devon, with its own mint, though it is now only a straggling village with much charm. In the Middle Ages it was a tin-mining centre, and the rather grim **Castle**, built in 1195, was used as a prison for unruly tin-miners. **St Petrock's Church** was built on the site of an early oratory, and contains some interesting 15th-c. stained glass, as well as a marvellous brass lectern. On the bank outside the church is a curious early 19th-c. gravestone to a clockmaker, George Routleigh, with the man's life described in clockmaking terms, and the churchyard is exceptionally rich in very old gravestones in excellent condition. *The Castle Inn* is a delightful old-fashioned place, with a surprising range of bar snacks and some interesting pictures of old Lydford.

To the W of the village, but badly signposted, is **Lydford Gorge** (NT), where the River Lyd descends for 2m over a series of swirling potholes, the most spectacular being The Devil's Cauldron. Footpaths lead alongside the gorge, and the 90ft-high waterfall known as The White Lady can be viewed.

Lynmouth and Lynton   1C
Towns on N coast (A39), 23m NE of Barnstaple. EC Thur. Inf: Tel (05985) 2225

Traditionally known as 'Little Switzerland', Lynmouth, by the sea, and Lynton, 600ft above it on the cliff-top, are surrounded by romantic wild scenery.

The two towns grew up at the confluence of two rivers, whose origins are in Exmoor: the East and West Lyn. In 1952 their peaceful wooded gorges brought disaster to Lynmouth: torrential flood waters which brought huge boulders crashing into the town. The flood cost 34 lives and the destruction of 90 houses, but since then the river bed has been widened and little trace of the dramatic events of the August night remain.

Of the twin-towns themselves, Lynmouth has the old-world appeal of thatched cottages and narrow streets (carefully restored after the flood) while Lynton is a Victorian town of considerable charm. They are united by a water-powered **Cliff Railway** opened in 1890. (The cars, which negotiate a height of 500ft, are linked by a steel cable and fitted with 700-gallon water tanks, filled at the top and emptied at the bottom.) An alternative way down to Lynmouth, other than by the road or railway, is a zig-zag cliff path, reached by North Walk, Lynton. In Lynton is the *Lyn and Exmoor Museum* (St Vincent's Cottage) which concentrates on Exmoor and local history: a special feature is an old country kitchen. The *Ancient Smithy* has a display of blacksmith's tools and equipment, and craftsmen can be seen at work in *Woodpecker Toys*.

The surrounding countryside can be enjoyed in a variety of walks. Most popular is the footpath walk along the cliffside to the **Valley of the Rocks**, 1m W, starting from North Walk, Lynton. (There is an alternative route over Hollerday Hill by a footpath behind the Town Hall.) These dramatically sited rock formations are mentioned in R.D. Blackmore's *Lorna Doone*. Now one of the sites of Devon's N coast, the massive pillars of rock are eroded into fantastic shapes: *Ragged Jack*, *The White Lady*, *The Devil's Cheesewring* are descriptive of a few. From the Valley of the Rocks, the walk can be extended W to *Lee Bay*.

From Lynmouth there are walks along the East and West Lyn Rivers. Footpaths start at the National Parks Information Centre. The East Lyn walk can be continued to *Watersmeet* (1¾m) an NT beauty spot at the meeting of the East Lyn River and Hoaroak Water, and from there to *Countisbury*. An alternative walk from Lynmouth is up the dramatic *Glen Lyn Gorge* which carried much of the flood water in the 1952 disaster: this is private and there is an admission fee.

Manaton　　　　3C
Dartmoor village on B3344, 3m S of Moretonhampstead, 10m NW of Newton Abbot

An absolutely unspoiled village with a green flanked by an avenue of trees. *St Winifred's Church* has some interesting 15th-c. stained glass, and close to the lychgate is an ancient thatched two-storey granite house, probably once the Church House. John Galsworthy, author of *The Forsyte Saga*, lived at Wingstone Farm 1906-23. Manaton is a good centre for exploring Dartmoor, and nearby is *Bowerman's Nose*, a curious pile of rocks named after a Mr Bowerman who was turned to stone by local witches when he crossed their path. Only his head (and hence nose) is above ground, for they buried him up to his neck. Also in the area are *Becky Falls* and *Grimspound*. (See also *Walk 6, p.26*.)

Marwood Hill Gardens　　　　1B
Gardens nr Marwood off B3230, 6m N of Barnstaple

A 5-acre private garden open to the public and specialising in camelias, rhododendrons, hydrangeas, and other flowering shrubs, set along winding paths bordering an attractive lake.

In the village, the *Church* has a magnificent 16th-c. screen, and on the S porch a sundial of 1762 which shows the time in Jerusalem, Berlin, Venice, Paris and – Marwood.

Mary Tavy　　　　3B
Dartmoor village on A386, 4m N of Tavistock

An interesting reminder of industrial Dartmoor, with the disused engine house and stack (known as *Wheal Betsy*) of the once prosperous copper, lead and silver mines, 1m N of the village. These were given to the NT in 1967.

Meavy　　　　3B
Dartmoor village off A386, 10m N of Plymouth

Adjoining the 13th-c. *St Peter's Church* are the remains of a manor house once lived in by Sir Francis Drake, but probably just as interesting is the ancient hollow oak tree in front of the church. There is evidence that it is about 1000 years old. It has a circumference of 27ft, and it is said that seven people once dined in it. *The Royal Oak Inn*, though not quite so old, is much more welcoming and comfortable.

Merrivale 3B
Dartmoor village on B3357, 5m E of Tavistock

Here can be seen the ruins of the ancient blowing house where tin miners smelted the ore in furnaces heated by bellows operated by a waterwheel. Channels were cut from the stream, and these leats can still be distinguished. Granite has also been quarried here, most recently for repairing Old London Bridge when it was moved to Arizona in 1968. The area is scattered with many Bronze Age hut circles, stone circles and enclosures.

Modbury 4B
Small town on A379, 12m E of Plymouth

A typical Devon hill town, with two impressive main streets flanked by imposing Georgian and Victorian houses. The choice of hostelries lies between the half-timbered *Exeter Inn*, dating back to 1563, and the 18th-c. *White Hart Hotel* with its colonnaded Assembly Rooms. Other fine buildings include the *Olde Traine House*, a 16th-c. farm, and the *Literary & Scientific Institution* (1840) in the Greek style with a fine cupola. The 14th-c. *Church* has fine tombs and a medieval spire that is a landmark of the area.

Molland 1C
Exmoor village off A361, 7m E of South Molton, 20m NW of Tiverton

The 15th-c. **St Mary's Church** has a near-perfect 18th-c. interior with a fascinating three-decker pulpit, box pews and screen with an 1808 rendering of the Ten Commandments. *Great Champson*, once a great house and now a farm, is worth a look, and nearby are disused copper and manganese mines. There is a 7m circular walk over Exmoor starting in the village. (See *Walk 9*, p.26.)

Bowerman's Nose

Moretonhampstead 3C

Small town on A382, 14m SE of Okehampton

A visitor of 1859 wrote that the small market town was 'swept by the purest and most invigorating breezes, and is remarkable for its salubrity, which the visitor may infer from the healthful look of the inhabitants, particularly the women who are quite Amazons in appearance.' Whether this is still true, today's visitors must judge for themselves. But Moretonhampstead is a very pretty town of well-maintained white-washed cottages. It is certainly worth exploring, if only for the views of the surrounding Dartmoor scenery. There is an attractive Market Square (triangular shaped) onto which faces the ancient *White Hart Inn*. The 15th-c. granite *St Andrew's Church* has a 90ft tower which cost 100s (£5) when it was built in 1418. Below it are the *Almshouses* (NT) of 1637, very solid looking with crudely turned pillars which gives them a marked medieval appearance. Also in Cross Street is *Mearsdon Manor*, a 13th-c. house with an 11th-c. doorway, and now a wildlife art gallery with a bird sanctuary in the garden.

The town is an excellent centre for walking tours: 15 minutes of brisk walking and the visitor is in wildest Dartmoor.

Mortehoe 1A/1B

Village on N coast off B3343, 6m W of Ilfracombe

Beautifully situated close to the treacherous Morte Point, where no less than five ships were wrecked in 1852, Mortehoe is an attractive village worth visiting for the early **Church of St Mary Magdalene** (12th-14th-c.). The building, which incorporates the local slate, retains three Norman doorways and a 13th-c. tower. Inside the church the carved bench ends are amongst the loveliest in Devon, and the tomb chest in the S transept to William de Tracy (d. 1322) should not be missed.

1m E of the village is the picturesque *Dammage Barton*, a farmhouse dating back to 1656 (not open). See also **Woolacombe* and *Walk 4*, p.25.

Morwellham Quay 3A

Village and industrial site off A390, 4m SW of Tavistock

Although only a riverside hamlet, Morwellham has been a port since Norman times, and became rich in the 19th c. when copper was found nearby and transported via the Tavistock Canal and down the Tamar to Plymouth. For a short while it became a boom-town, and the 'greatest copper mine and port in Queen Victoria's Empire' but then the copper ran out and the village reverted to quiet seclusion. However it is being restored, and there are now fascinating exhibits including a riverside tramway which goes inside the old copper mine, a raised railway and blacksmith's, copper's, assayer's and chandler's workshops. The former *Ship Inn* has been converted into tea-rooms.

Newton Abbot 3C

Pop 19,400. 16m SW of Exeter (A380). Events: Carnival Week, (last week in Jul); Cheese and Onion Fair (2nd week in Sep). EC Thur MD Wed & Sat. Inf: Tel (0626) 67494

A new town in the 12th c. belonging to Torre Abbey in Torquay (hence its name), Newton Abbot was made rich by the wool and leather trades, and as a transport centre for the handling of granite from Dartmoor. The arrival of the railway in 1846 did much to promote the town. From the railway period date the steep terraces of brick working men's houses, and the larger middle-class villas which characterise the town. Almost nothing pre-Victorian remains in the town centre except for the 14th-c. **St Leonard's Tower** (the church was demolished last century) which now serves as a traffic island and is the town's symbol.

The town is famous for its Wednesday and Saturday **Markets**, possibly the liveliest in Devon, when in addition to livestock a great range of local produce is available from the many stalls. There is also an extensive antique market held every Tuesday in East Street, attracting dealers from many parts of the West Country.

About 1m E of the centre on the Torquay Road is *Ford House* (1610) where Charles I and William of Orange both stayed. It is at present being restored and converted to council offices. ¾m W of the centre on the Totnes Road (A381) are some fine Victorian *Almshouses* and a little further on the other side (not visible from the road) is **Bradley Manor** (NT), a fine 15th-c. manor house with a great hall, chapel and kitchen.

Newton Abbot is ideally placed as a base for Dartmoor, with the National Park Headquarters 5m N at Bovey Tracey.

Newton Ferrers   4B
Village on B3186, 7m SE of Plymouth

An old fishing village on the N side of a creek of the Yealm estuary, facing *Noss Mayo* on the S bank, the village is now a haven for yachtsmen. 1½m SE of the village down the coast is the old *Church*, deserted in the 19th c. and now a picturesque ruin given over to the elements. (See also *Walk 1*, p.25.)

North Bovey   3C
Dartmoor village off A382, 2m SW of Moretonhampstead

Reached only by twisting narrow tree-girt lanes, North Bovey is a beautiful little village surrounding a picture-postcard village green, with white-washed houses, prize-winning cottage gardens and a 15th-c. granite *Church*. *The Ring of Bells* is a very attractive inn dating from the 13th c. *Manor Hotel*, 1m N, was originally North Bovey Manor, built in 1907 regardless of expense. North Bovey is a perfect base to explore this delightful part of Dartmoor.

North Molton   1C
Village off A361, 3m N of South Molton

Once enriched by the gold and copper that was mined around here, North Molton is now a sleepy neighbour to the larger and livelier *South Molton*. A number of buildings, however, testify to the former wealth of the village. **All Saints' Church** has a fine alabaster monument (1626) to the local mine-owning landlord, Sir Amyas Bamfylde, his wife and 17 children; also a splendid

medieval pulpit. Near the church are the *Court House* (1553) and Georgian *Court Hall*. One active industry is the *Malthouse Pottery*, open to visitors.

Noss Mayo
See *Newton Ferrers*

Okehampton   2B
Town on A30, 23m W of Exeter Event: Town Show (Aug). EC Wed MD Sat. Nat Park Inf Centre: Tel (0837) 3020

The most dramatic view of Oke-hampton is from the N, with the high ground of NE Dartmoor beyond. The town itself is not especially impressive, its only buildings of merit the *Town Hall* (1685) in Fore Street and the Georgian *White Hart*, a former coaching inn, opposite. Of the 15th-c. *Church* only the granite tower survived a fire in the last century: the Victorian successor has windows by William Morris. In an old mill off West Street the **Museum of Dartmoor Life** shows how people used to live and work on Dartmoor, with domestic and mining exhibits.

On the river S of the town are the ruins of what was once the largest and most important castle in Devon. Built by the Normans in the 11th c. and largely reconstructed for the Court-enays (Earls of Devon) in the 14th c., **Okehampton Castle** was abandoned after 1537 when Henry VIII, unsure of the loyalty of the local nobility, beheaded the Earl of Devon and dismantled the building.

To the N of the town is *Oaklands* (1830) a fine Grecian-style mansion. ¾m to the SE is *Okehampton Camp*, an Iron Age fortification overlooking the river Oakment, and 4m to the S are *Yes Tor* (2031ft) and *High Willhays* (2038ft), the highest points on Dartmoor and therefore in S England. When not covered in the ubiquitous Dartmoor mists, there are stunning views for many miles over Dartmoor, to the N towards Exmoor, and W towards Bodmin Moor.

4m E on the A30 is *Sticklepath*, with its Museum of Rural Industry.

Ottery St Mary 2D
Small town off A30, 12m E of Exeter. Event:
Carnival and Tar Barrel Rolling (Nov 5)

With its quaint old shops and air of having been bypassed by the modern age, this town has great appeal. It is clustered around the magnificent **St Mary's Church**, one of the finest in Devon. Although the core of the church is 13th-c., the greatest glories are the 14th-c. nave with its superb painted roof, Lady Chapel and transeptal towers modelled on Exeter Cathedral. The latter were built by Bishop Grandisson, who made sure his family was remembered with a noble canopied tomb (1358). Also not to be missed are the *Dorset Aisle* of 1520 with its beautiful fan-vaulted roof and the 600-year-old clock, one of the four oldest in Britain. The weather vane on top of the church is unusual: it whistles in the wind. The poet Samuel Taylor Coleridge, who wrote *The Rhyme of the Ancient Mariner*, was born in the vicarage. An interesting relic of the Industrial Revolution is the *Serge Factory* (1788-90). There are delightful walks along the river Otter, and 1m N is *Cadhay House*.

Paignton 4C
Pop 35,000. 27m S of Exeter (A379). EC Wed.
Inf: Tel (0803) 558383

Somewhat in the shadow of its neighbour Torquay, Paignton sprang to life in Victorian times with the coming of the railway, and is a most popular family resort with a fine sandy beach, a pier 800ft long, and entertainments for all, including the extensive **Zoo** (75 acres) on the Totnes Road. The town is well served with parks, with the usual facilities for golf, putting, and impromptu cricket and football. There is a small but well-stocked *aquarium* near the charming little harbour.

St John's Church is 15th-c. but on Saxon foundations, which shows that Paignton is much older than might at first appear. It boasts a fine Norman door and the glorious 15th-c. *Kirkham Chantry*, a masterpiece of medieval carving. Next to the church is the pink sandstone *Coverdale Tower*, the scant remains of the old Bishop of Exeter's Palace.

Kirkham House in Kirkham Street is an interesting example of a 14th-c. stone house, and is open to the public, though it is sparsely furnished and rather bleak. This cannot be said of the vast **Oldway Mansion** at the centre of town, the result of an attempt by the millionaire Singer sewing-machine family to establish a lavish French château in Devon with 115 rooms and no expense spared. There is a huge ballroom, suites copied from Versailles and 6 acres of elaborate gardens. Beautifully kept by the local council, there are few restrictions on wandering around what are in effect council offices, though

earnest visitors looking for a rent rebate may well imagine that they have wandered onto a film set with Gloria Swanson ready to descend the massive marble staircase. Nearby are *Compton Castle, *Berry Pomeroy Castle, and the *Torbay Aircraft Museum. A stretch of the *Dart Valley Railway runs between Paignton and *Kingswear.

Parracombe
1B
Village off A39, 7m SW of Lynton, 13m NE of Barnstaple

Approached by way of a steep hill, Parracombe is a delightful village, the old parish church of which, **St Petrock**, is particularly worth a visit (reached by continuing 1/4m W along the A39 past the turning to the village and turning right). Made redundant in 1878 when a new church closer to the village was built, it was spared the indignity of Victorian 'restoration' and is one of the few West Country churches with an unspoiled Georgian interior. It still has the (draught-resisting) box pews, text-boards over the screen, pulpit with painted canopy and hat pegs for the local farmers. Just above the village are the bare remains of *Holwell Castle*, once an important Norman fortification. 2m W, in Cowley Wood, is the *Cowley Cleave Nature Trail*, open from Mar-Dec, a pleasant 1m stroll through mixed woodland with the opportunity to birdwatch from a hide.

PLYMOUTH

*building, etc. of outstanding interest

Population 249,800

Tourist information Civic Centre. Tel (0752) 264849. Also 12 The Barbican, Tel (0752) 23806. Mon-Sat 9-5.30

EC Wed **MD** Mon-Sat

Events Lord Mayor's Day (May), Plymouth Navy Days (Aug Bank Hol)

Places of interest
All places listed are open to the public and described in the text that follows

Churches

St Andrew Finewell Street

Historic Buildings

***The Elizabethan House** New Street, The Barbican
Mon-Sat 10-1 & 2.15-6 (4.30 in winter) also Apr-Sep Sun 3-5

The Merchant's House St Andrew's Street
Mon-Sat 10-6, Sun 3-5

Mount Edgcumbe House Cremyll
House: May-Sep Mon, Tue 2-6; park all year in daylight

Prysten House Finewell Street
Mon-Sat 10-4

***The Royal Citadel** Madeira Road
May-Sep, tours daily 2, 3, 4 & 5

***Smeaton's Tower** The Hoe
May-Sep, 10.30 – 1hr before dusk

Museum

City Museum and Art Gallery Drake Circus
Mon-Sat 10-6

Historic Inns
See p.23

Other places of interest

Aquarium The Hoe
Mon-Sat 10-6

Drake's Island The Sound
Ferry from Mayflower Steps, The Barbican, May-Sep 10-4 on the hr

Sutton Harbour, Plymouth

Now the largest town W of Bristol, Plymouth had inauspicious beginnings as a village (named Sutton) owned by Plympton Abbey. It rose to prominence in the 13th c., when it acquired its present name, and was used as a port for assembling fleets against the French. Since that time it has always been one of Britain's most important naval centres. Sir Francis Drake sailed around the world from Plymouth, and with other 'adventurers' like Hawkins and Frobisher, attacked Spanish booty ships from Plymouth. Their attacks culminated in the Spanish Armada of 1588. Drake is supposed to have played bowls on The Hoe while watching the Spanish fleet sail past (with his own navy safely hidden out of sight) before sailing out to rout them.

In 1620 the Pilgrim Fathers sailed for Newfoundland from Plymouth and

The Hoe This green prominence in the centre of Plymouth is a cross between a public park and a military parade ground. It commands magnificent views over *Plymouth Sound* and W over Cornwall. Just offshore from The Hoe can be seen *Drake's Island*, once a military fortress and prison but now a youth adventure centre (reached by ferry from Sutton Harbour). Beyond it 3m out is the *Breakwater*, 1m long with a fortress in the centre and a lighthouse at the W end, created 1812-1844 from 3½ million tons of stone to make Plymouth a safe harbour in any weather. 17m out, visible only on a clear day or at night is the *Eddystone Lighthouse*. The first lighthouse in the world stood here from 1698 until it was washed away by a storm five years later. The second burnt down, and the one now operating is the fourth. The third is *Smeaton's Tower*, built in 1769 and moved to The Hoe in 1882 following the erosion of the rock on which it stood. It is now probably Plymouth's best-known landmark. Also on The Hoe is the dignified *War Memorial* to the naval dead of both World Wars, an *Armada Memorial*, a popular *Statue of Drake* (by Boehm 1884), and a bowling green – maintaining Drake's tradition to this day.

On the E side of The Hoe is the **Royal Citadel**, a five-sided stone and granite fortress built by Charles II (1666-71). Because the town had been strongly Parliamentarian in the Civil War, the King had cannons ranged over the town as well as out to sea. Within the massive walls (nearly 1m long) are some of the original Carolean buildings including the *Royal Chapel of St Katherine* (enlarged last century) which has a lovely interior with three wooden galleries. The Citadel stands on the site of an earlier fort built here by Sir Francis Drake after the defeat of the Armada. From the battlements one can look down on the old harbour (Sutton Harbour) where Drake held his fleet before the attack on the Armada.

W of the Citadel, by the Hoe, is Plymouth's *Aquarium*.

many other expeditions, central to Britain's history, have started in Plymouth, including James Cook's discovery of Australia in 1772, and Darwin's expedition to the South Seas in *The Beagle*. In 1919 the first transatlantic flight ended in Plymouth, and most recently much of the Falklands Task Force left from the naval dockyards at Devonport in the Sound.

Because of its naval importance Plymouth was a major target for German bombing in the last war. However, some of the oldest parts were not hit, and the redevelopment has not been as damaging as in many cities. Plymouth now divides into four major parts: The Hoe, which faces out to sea, the Barbican area around the (old) Sutton Harbour, the new Shopping Centre and the Devonport Docks.

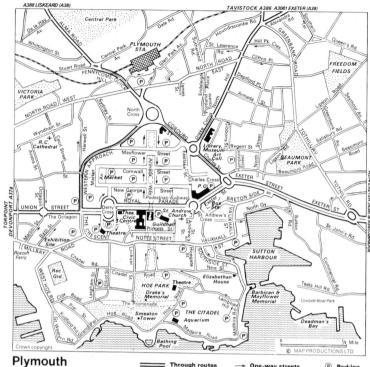

Plymouth

━━━━ **Through routes**   → **One-way streets**   Ⓟ **Parking**

E of The Hoe, and built around Sutton Harbour is **The Barbican**, the city's 'historic quarter'. Here the streets follow the medieval pattern, and many of the buildings are 300-500 years old.

Starting at the *Mayflower Steps*, from where the Pilgrim Fathers sailed for New England in 1620, you can see *Sutton Harbour*, which was the main port until the development of Devonport from 1691. On the quay is *Island House* where the Pilgrim Fathers stayed before sailing. On the side of the house is a plaque which lists all those who sailed: there were no women!

Up the hill from the house runs *New Street*. At no 32 is the **Elizabethan House**, a delightful Tudor house well-furnished with period furniture. Further up the street on the same side at No 40 is a secret *Elizabethan Garden*

(open 9-5) hidden behind the buildings.

At the brow of the hill turn down Pin Lane to Southside Street, turn left and pass the *Coates Black Friars Distillery*, now part of a gin distillery, but one of the oldest buildings in Plymouth, dating back to 1430 when it was the hall to a priory. It was later used as a debtor's prison. Continue to the end of Southside Street and turn left into Notte Street and first right into St Andrew's Street. At its top end is the **Merchant's House**, a very fine 16th-c. half-timbered and limestone house. It was built by William Parker, a typical Plymouth hero. He was a privateer who twice raided the Spanish treasure fleet and became rich on the proceeds. For his success he was made Mayor in 1601 and died at sea on another expedition in 1618. Behind the house is Finewell

80

Street, and at its top end is the **Prysten House**, a splendid 15th-c. stone building with a central galleried courtyard. The house was built by Plympton Priory for Augustinian priests.

Opposite the Prysten House is the parish *Church of St Andrew*, built in the 15th c. but gutted in the 1941 bombing. It has been restored and is rather dull but for the striking modern glass by John Piper. Next to the church, (to the W) is the Victorian *Guildhall*. Beyond it is the Civic Centre, a 13-storey building with a viewing platform offering panoramic views of the city and Sound.

Due N of The Hoe and centred on *Armada Way* is the new **Shopping Centre**, entirely rebuilt since the war. It contains a covered market which operates six days a week and almost every major chain store. Parking facilities are good by inner-city standards. To its NE side, at Drake Circus, is the *City Museum and Art Gallery*, with collections of Egyptiana, local history and geology and a very fine collection of 17th-18th c. portraits by Van Dyck, Kneller, Lely and Reynolds. SE of Drake Circus is *Charles Church*, once a fine Jacobean Gothic church, but destroyed by bombs in 1941. It has been left as a shell as a memorial to the 366 Plymouth civilians killed in the last war.

The **Royal Devonport Docks** are still the navy's major port, and for that reason are not open to them the public. However, good views of them can be obtained from the *Tamar Ferry* on the A374, from Torpoint where it lands or from a boat trip around the dockyards (summer only) leaving from Phoenix Wharf near the Mayflower Steps.

Technically in Cornwall, but closer to Plymouth than anywhere else is *Mount Edgcumbe*, a Tudor mansion and 800 acres of landscaped park with superb views of Plymouth and the Sound.

Plymouth is one of the best sporting centres in the country with the finest sailing and windsurfing, swimming, tennis, golf and deep sea fishing. For a beautiful coast walk in the area, see *Walk 1*, p.25.

Plympton   4B
Town on A374, 3m E of Plymouth

Now regarded as a dormitory town for Plymouth, the two Plymptons – of St Maurice and St Mary – were once much more important than their majestic neighbour (then called Sutton). Traces of this survive in the ruins of the Norman *Castle* (dismantled after battles in the Civil War) and the fine buildings in Fore Street including the *Guildhall* (1690) and *Grammar School* (1658). Sir Joshua Reynolds, the first President of the Royal Academy and Britain's greatest portrait painter was brought up in Plympton where his father was vicar and headmaster. Both Plymptons have interesting churches, but the 14th and 15th-c. *St Mary* is particularly fine with an impressive tomb (1464) and 14th-c. windows and piscina. 1m SE is *Saltram House*.

Poltimore   2D
Village off B3181, 5m NE of Exeter

This early Victorian village was the brain child of the Bampfylde family who were very important hereabouts and whose monuments can be seen in the *Church*, which has a squire's pew in the S gallery complete with a private fireplace. Just N of the church are the *Almshouses* of 1631, with medallions of their benefactors, again the Bampfyldes. The Georgian *Poltimore House*, now a nursing home, is plain but imposing.

Postbridge   3B
Dartmoor village on B3212, 21m NE of Plymouth. Nat Park Inf Centre: Tel (0822) 88220

An oasis in the rugged grandeur of Dartmoor, Postbridge was once an important place but is now merely a handful of cottages. It is the site of the best **clapper bridge** on Dartmoor – 42ft long and standing 7ft above the East Dart River. Some historians claim it is Bronze Age, while others think it dates only from the 13th c. when it would have been used by the pack-horses carrying tin and wool. 2m S is *Bellever Bridge* of similar construction, but dating from only 1728. The area around Postbridge is crowded with prehistoric

Clapper bridge at Postbridge

stone circles, enclosures and hut circles. Traces can also be found of the long disused *Vitifer tin and copper mines*.

2m NW on the B3212 is *The Warren House Inn*, where a peat fire has been burning continually for over 130 years. A tough 13m walk starts and finishes at the inn. (See *Walk 8*, p.26.)

Powderham Castle   3D
Castle on river Exe off A379, 8m S of Exeter

One of Devon's finest country mansions, Powderham has belonged to the Courtenay family since 1377. The building dates from the 14th c., with additions over the centuries, though the overall look of the house today reflects the Victorian rebuilding of 1840-45. The rooms are well furnished and adorned with fine paintings, and include a handsome domed music room by James Wyatt (1790s). There is a lively programme of events in the grounds, including vintage car rallies. The gardens and park are splendidly laid out, and one of the few remaining deer herds in Devon can be seen in idyllic surroundings. A Belvedere

dating from 1773 is in the grounds, and in Pigeon Vale nearby is a cottage cleverly converted from an old dovecote.

Princetown   3B
Small town on B3212, 8m E of Tavistock. Nat Park Inf Centre: Tel (082289) 414

Described in 1859 as 'one of the most gaunt and dreary places imaginable', Princetown is not without interest to the visitor. It is situated on the bleakest part of Dartmoor, 1400ft above sea level, and has a military look that matches the grim *Prison*. It was built in 1806 and used first for French and then American prisoners-of-war. More than 200 American prisoners died here, leading a contemporary Frenchman to comment that: 'It is truly Siberia, covered with unmelting snow; when the snows go away, the mists appear. Imagine the tyranny of perfidious Albion in sending human beings to such a place.' The present prison dates from about 1850, and although inmates have escaped from time to time they do not last long on the moors. Many of the quarries worked by convicts can be seen nearby. Today it is no longer a high security gaol, though it is certainly the most forbidding prison in the country. Needless to say there is no public admission – nor are visitors encouraged to stop and look. But they are welcome at *The Plume of Feathers*, a popular inn, much older than the prison.

River Dart Country Park 3C
On B3357, 2m NW of Ashburton

A country park with woodland and riverside walks, picnic meadows, and nature trails. There are facilities for fly-fishing, swimming and pony-riding. Children are catered for with an extensive adventure playground with Tarzan swings, rope bridges and pony rides.

Rosemoor Gardens 2B
Gardens on B3220, 1m S of Great Torrington, 26m N of Okehampton

A charming private garden started in 1959 and open to the public. Noted for its rare trees, rhododendrons, primulas and roses.

Salcombe 4C
Town on S coast (A381), 28m SE of Plymouth. EC Thur. Inf: Tel (054884) 2736

This idyllic resort is the most southerly in Devon and has one of the mildest climates in England; even oranges and lemons grow along the estuary. It is an enchanting sailing centre, has first-rate restaurants, an intricate one-way road system, and marvellous views across the estuary. From the tiny harbour boats can be hired by the hour at low cost, and it is ideal for beginners, as the estuary is very safe. By the waters are the ruins of *Salcombe Castle* (Fort Charles), built by Henry VIII as a defence against the French and used by the Royalists in the Civil War.

1½m SW at Sharpitor, set in 6 acres of lovely gardens planted by Otto Overbeck (d. 1937) is **Overbecks** (NT), a museum which contains an admirable collection of furniture, embroideries and local material about ships, wrecks and shipbuilding.

Across the estuary are some of the best and least frequented sandy beaches in the county. The reason for their neglect is that to get to them by road necessitates a wide detour up-river and across the bay, (although there is a passenger ferry across the bay). There is a stupendous coastal path walk to *Bolt Head* (3m) and on to *Bolt Tail* (8m) along the black cliff-tops; a 5m circular tour starting at Sharpitor takes in Bolt Head (See *Walk 2*, p.25.) This wild stretch of coast has taken its toll of ships, including one from the Spanish Armada (1588), a frigate with 500 people aboard in 1760, and a famous windjammer in 1936.

Saltram House (NT) 4B
Historic house off A38, 3m E of Plymouth

One of Devon's finest country mansions, with interiors by Robert Adam. The original Tudor house at the core of the building was purchased by George Parker (ancestor of the Earls of Morley) in 1712. Most of the existing Georgian building was created by his son (from 1743) and grandson (from 1768). The latter, John Parker II, was a friend of Sir Joshua Reynolds, who was educated in nearby *Plympton. The Doric porch (1818) was the house's last addition, leaving us with a perfect period piece.

The interior decoration is the finest example of Robert Adam's work in the south-west. The entrance hall and morning room have richly stuccoed ceilings, and the latter is graced by fine 18th-c. paintings, including five portraits by Reynolds. The grand saloon and dining room retain Adam's work in its entirely, from the Axminster carpets, echoing the design of the ceilings, to the door-handles and mirrors. Other delights are the Mirror Room, hung with Chinese mirror paintings, the library and the Chinese Chippendale bedroom. The Victorian kitchen, with its elaborate hot water system, was in use until 1963.

In the splendid landscaped *Park* are various 18th-c. buildings: an octagonal 'Gothick' – style summer, an orangery and a disused chapel.

Shaldon 3C
Village on A379 on S bank of Teign estuary opp.
Teignmouth, 7m N of Torquay

Although only across the river from Teignmouth, Shaldon belongs to a different world, with fishermen's cottages and box-like Regency houses fronted by pretty gardens. The narrow main street runs parallel with the river estuary, with fine views of Teignmouth. Shaldon is a noted sailing centre, and has its own secluded beach reached by a cliff tunnel (*Smuggler's Cave*). The *Shaldon Wildlife Collection* has exotic birds, mammals and reptiles.

Sandford 2C
Village 2m N of intersection of A3072 & A377 at
Crediton

This attractive village is in one of the most fertile parishes in Devon. The 15th-c. **St Swithin's Church** has a notable carved Jacobean W Gallery (1657) and old oak pews, with fine carved bench ends. The most impressive building in the village, however, is the **School** of 1825, with heavy Tuscan pillars and pedimented windows. *Shoplands Pottery* in New Building produces a wide range of items.

Saunton Sands see *Braunton*

Seaton 4D
Town on S coast (B3174), 10m E of Sidmouth.
EC Thur. Inf: Tel (0297) 21660

A very fresh, slightly superior town at the mouth of the River Axe, with traces of Roman occupation. There are fine pebble beaches, and superb cliff walks in both directions, E towards Lyme Regis going over the *Great Landslip* of 1839 (which locals thought presaged the end of the world) and W to *Beer* and *Branscombe* (5m). Seaton is well served for bowling greens, tennis courts, putting greens, children's swimming and paddling pools, and the world's last electric open-air tram (**Seaton & District Electric Tramway**) which runs along the River Axe between Seaton and *Colyton*. Beachcombers will have fun looking for garnets, beryls, agates, jasper, cornelians and other stones.

Shebbear 2A
Village off A388, 9m NE of Holsworthy

This remote village in Devon's rural heartland has much to offer visitors. The 800-year-old **St Michael's Church** has an impressive Norman door with carved faces. Inside are some interesting monuments, and in the churchyard, under an ancient oak tree, is the *Devil's Stone*. Here, it is popularly believed, the devil sleeps for 364 days a year: on the remaining day, November 5th, all the men in the village turn the stone to briefly release him.

The *Shebbear Pottery* offers a look at potters in action. 2m NE of the village is the *Alscott Farm Museum*, which contains a collection of vintage tractors, ploughs and other farm equipment.

Sheepstor 3B
Dartmoor village off B3212, 13m NE of Plymouth

Splendidly situated between granite rocks and the beautifully landscaped *Burrator Reservoir* – Sheepstor is a lovely quiet village. In the churchyard is a huge red Aberdeen granite sarcophagus, a memorial to the 'White Rajah of Sarawak', Sir James Brooke, who retired to Burrator House and died there in 1868. (The grave of his successor Sir Charles Brooke is also in the churchyard). Inside the church is the delightful alabaster memorial to Elizabeth Elford who died in 1641. ½m N on the shores of the reservoir are the ruins of *Elford Manor House*, and on Sheepstor itself above the village is an ancient cave believed to be inhabited by 'piskies'.

Sidmouth 3D
Pop 11,890. 15m E of Exeter (A3052). Event:
Folklore Festival (1st week in Aug). EC Thur
Inf: Tel (03955) 6441

Finely situated on the estuary of the River Sid between the red sandstone cliffs of Salcombe Hill and Peak Hill, Sidmouth is a charming enclave of Regency architecture, with royal associations. Queen Victoria spend some time as a girl at the castellated Woolbrook Cottage (now the *Royal Glen Hotel*, and full of period character). The exceptionally wide *Esplanade* flanked by delightful cottages with verandas, dates from 1837, and the shops have an air of a bygone age, short on supermarkets and long on old-fashioned purveyors to the gentry. Sidmouth has an enchanting *Museum* (Hope Cottage, Church Street), with a collection of toys and dolls and items of local interest. Here the visitor will discover that until about 1450 when the harbour silted up, Sidmouth was a port of importance.

The finest beach is *Jacob's Ladder* (so called because it is reached by a wooden ladder) centred around a tiny hillock just W of the town centre, on which there is a fairy-tale cottage. Unusually for Devon seaside resorts, Sidmouth boasts a cricket ground up to County standards and 2m NE on *Salcombe Hill* is an observatory, founded in 1912 and sometimes open to the public. At Slade Farm, just to the E of Salcombe Regis, is the *Donkey Sanctuary*, a charity for retired donkeys which is open to the public.

There is an agreeable walk from Sidmouth alongside the river N to Sidford through fields called *The Byes*, and for the more ambitious there is the *South West Coast Path*, W to *Budleigh Salterton* (8m), or E to *Branscombe* (5m) and *Beer* (9m).

Slapton Ley   4C
Nature Reserve on S coast (A379), 7m E of Kingsbridge

A lake (or ley) of about 200 acres, part of Slapton Ley Nature Reserve. Rich in birdlife, it is separated from the sea by a narrow strip of shingle and is well stocked with freshwater fish. Angling by boat is allowed, though fishermen should book beforehand (054858) 466. See also *Torcross*.

South Molton   1C
Town on A361, 12m SE of Barnstaple. Event: Annual Sheep Fair (end Aug). EC Wed & Sat, MD Thur

An 8th-c. Anglo-Saxon settlement, South Molton owed its later prosperity to the wool trade, the coaching route (Taunton-Barnstaple) and its proximity to the iron and copper mines of *North Molton*. These activities have either disappeared or declined and it is now a farming town with a regular livestock market.

The long High Street swells out into the Market Place, and there are a number of interesting buildings, including on the S side the *Guildhall* (1740-3) and *Market House* (1863), both in the Italian style. In the centre of Broad Street is the curiously named *Medical Hall* (now a chemist) with its iron verandah and heavy columns. There are some delightful Georgian houses and shops, and the Guildhall has a *Museum* of local history and a comprehensive collective of weights and measures. The approach to the 15th-c. *Church* is through a large cast-iron gate opposite the Guildhall. Inside are some fine carvings of figures on the pulpit and the columns of the aisles.

South West Coast Path
N coast & S coast

From Minehead in Somerset to Dorset, the South West Coast Path extends through Devon and Cornwall for 512m. It is the country's longest footpath with stupendous cliff, beach and coastal scenery. Throughout its length it is well marked by special signposts with the emblem of an acorn or the initials S.W.C.P. or 'Devon Coast Path'. It is generally well-made but in some places there are scrambles. A number of detailed guides to different stretches of the path are available from local bookshops and tourist information offices. For five different circular walks incorporating some of the best stretches of the Path, see *Walks 1-5*, p.25.

South Zeal   3B
Dartmoor village off A30, 5m E of Okehampton

At the heart of the village is the T-shaped *Oxenham Arms Inn*, an early Tudor building with mullioned windows. The former manor of the Burgoyne family, the inn is mentioned in Charles Kingsley's novel *Westward Ho!* At the upper end of the village street is the *Chapel* dated 1713, but considered to be much earlier, and behind an ancient weathered cross. The area around is rich in medieval farmhouses, among the most interesting *West Week*, *Oxenham* and *Wickington*.

Spinster's Rock 3B
Ancient monument on A382, 7m E of Okehampton and 1m S of intersection with A30

The impressive Spinster's Rock is an ancient burial place comprising a huge granite slab supported by three uprights. Local folklore has it that the monument was erected one morning by three old spinsters before breakfast! In fact it is a Neolithic tomb about 5-6000 years old.

Spreyton 2B
Dartmoor village off A30, 9m E of Okehampton

The delightful 15th-c. *Church* in this remote moorland village is approached by a tall avenue of limes. An inscription around the barrel roof commemorates Henry le Maygne, vicar in 1451. More famous is the *Tom Cobley Tavern* (licensed 1589). A sign in the inn says:

> From this village of Spreyton on
> a day in September 1802, the
> following left for Widdecombe
> Fair, Bill Brewer, Dan Stewer,
> Peter Gurney, Peter Davy, Dan'l
> Widden, Harry Hawke, and
> Uncle Tom Cobley and All.

Starcross 3D
Village on River Exe and A379, 11m S of Exeter

Fronting the estuary of the Exe and a fine base for sailing, Starcross is a pretty village famous for the ill-fated *Atmospheric Railway* invented by Isambard Kingdom Brunel. The trains, which were fast, quiet and a very smooth ride were 'pushed' along by air pressure with a plunger in a metal pipe that ran along the tracks. Unfortunately the valves were made of greased leather and rats gnawed through them, bringing the trains to a halt. All that remains of this brave experiment is one pumping house and *The Atmospheric Railway Inn* in the village. A passenger ferry connects Starcross with *Exmouth* and 1m to the N is *Powderham Castle*.

Start Point Lighthouse 4C
Coastal promontory, 12m S of Dartmouth, 3m S of A379

An exhilirating walk from the lost village of *Hallsands*, the lighthouse, on a dramatic promontory, is 94ft high. It shows two lights, a red one warning ships of the dangerous reefs, and the traditional light flashing three times every ten seconds. There is a spectacular stretch of the *South West Coast Path* from Start Point W to Lannacombe, passing Matchcombe Cove with its curious pillars on the sands, a distance of about 3m.

Staverton 4C
Village off A384, 4m NW of Totnes. Event: Annual Raft Race (Aug)

The *Church of St Paul de Leon* (1330-50) has a fine screen and interesting brasses, and the *Sea Trout Inn* is celebrated. But the real interest of the village is the **bridge** with its splendid river views (½m N of the church). It was built in 1413 with seven arches and pedestrian bays by the local bishop who financed it by selling Indulgences (worth 40 days remission in Purgatory) to all who contributed towards the cost. It is a good place to view the annual raft race down the Dart held each August. Staverton is one of the stops of the *Dart Valley Railway*, and some of the rolling stock is kept here out of season to the delight of steam-railway enthusiasts.

At *Riverford Farm*, a working farm, there is a wagon tour, and all kinds of farm animals can be viewed at close quarters.

Sticklepath 2B
Dartmoor village on A30, 5m E of Okehampton

A straggling village of squat little cottages, containing the award-winning **Finch Foundry Trust and Sticklepath Museum of Rural Industry**, a 19th-c. foundry with water-powered machinery including two enormous tilt hammers and a wooden aqueduct. Sticklepath has always been an important centre of Non-Conformity, and Quakers from the village were amongst the very first settlers of Pennsylvania. John Wesley, the founder of Methodism, preached here often and the *Quaker Burial Ground* (opened 1713) is still a peaceful haven. To the W of the village is *The Rising Sun*, an inn famous for its bar snacks and home-made steak pies.

Stoke Gabriel 4C
Village on River Dart off A385, 6m SE of Totnes

A delightful small village on the Dart estuary, with an intricate street system and a very old church, *St Mary and St Gabriel*, noteworthy for its ancient yew in the churchyard, probably 1000-1500 years old. The church retains a 15th-c. screen and pulpit. The *Lotus Pottery* is open to visitors during normal shop hours.

Swimbridge 1B
Village on A361, 5m SE of Barnstaple

The village is named after Sawin of Birage, the priest who founded **St James's Church** in the time of Edward the Confessor. His church has gone, but the existing building of *c.* 1310 (with 15th and 16th-c. additions) is of great interest. It has the finest medieval spire in N Devon (14th-c., lead shingled) and inside are fabulous carvings on the roof bosses (15th-c.), a beautiful rood screen and ornate Renaissance font cover and canopy. The stone pulpit is 15th-c. Jack Russell, the founder of the breed of terriers that bears his name, was vicar here in the 19th c.

Tapeley Park 1B
Historic house off A39 nr Instow, 2m NW of Bideford

Commanding splendid views of the Taw and Torridge estuaries, this elegant house was purchased in the early 18th c. by the Cleveland family. The brick façade was added to the original William and Mary house in the 1850s after the house had passed by marriage to the Christie family of Glyndebourne fame. (The last male Cleveland, Archibald, was killed in 1854 at the Battle of Inkerman). The interior still has some of the original ceilings and a good collection of furniture, including pieces by William Morris. The house owes its present appearance to Lady Rosamond Christie,

grandmother of the present owner, who commissioned John Belcher to restore it at the beginning of the century. Belcher added the porticoes and created the Italian gardens in the early 1900s. These gardens were laid out in formal style with pond, grotto, old walled kitchen garden and brick ice-house. The stables at the rear of the house have been made into an attractive tea room.

Tavistock 3B
Town on A386, 15m N of Plymouth. Events: Carnival (May) Goose Fair (2nd week Oct) EC Wed MD Wed, Fri Nat Park Info Centre: Tel (0822) 2938

One of the medieval Stannary towns (administrative centres for Dartmoor's tin mines) Tavistock was also a prosperous wool centre. Symbol of its importance was the Abbey, founded in 974. This was destroyed after the Dissolution and the Abbey and the town became the property of the Russell family, later the Dukes of Bedford. Tavistock's greatest son was Francis Drake, born in 1542 at Crowndale Farm (1m SW, house now vanished). 19th-c. copper mining notably at *Mary Tavy* and *Lamerton* brought further prosperity to the town, but these mines were abandoned at the turn of the century. Tavistock is now an agricultural town with a weekly cattle market (Wed), and is a shopping and tourist centre for Dartmoor.

The town owes much of its building to the Dukes of Bedford, who built the castellated stone *Bedford Hotel* (*c.* 1820) and in 1860 the *Town Hall, Guildhall* and *Pannier Markets* at the centre of the town, in the inevitably named Bedford Square. The Guildhall incorporates part of the W gate of the Abbey (of which little else survives). This attractive ensemble, together with the Victorian shop fronts of *Duke Street* and *West Street* and the smart Bedford Villas in the Plymouth Road, are a perfect example of Victorian town building at its best. The Dukes were also responsible for the erection of the *Statue of Drake* (1883) at the W end of the town on the Plymouth Road. The statue was so popular that a copy was made in Plymouth.

Built by the tin-workers in the 15th c., the parish **Church of St Eustace** has a lofty tower, the town's principal landmark. The church contains a fine alabaster monument to Judge John Glanville and his wife, and there is a **William Morris** window. In the churchyard is an arch from the cloisters of the old Abbey.

To transport the town's tin to the Tamar, the Tavistock Canal was built (1803-17) from the Meadows – now the town park – to *Morwellham Quay*, 4m SW. Unfortunately the tin supplies ran out in the 1870s.

Tawstock   1B
Village off B3232, 2m S of Barnstaple

A charming village with an early 14th-c. church of unusual interest, **St Peter's**. The structure has been little altered in 500 years except that it is filled with splendid monuments to the mighty Earls of Bath (and their wives) who were lords of the manor here. Their grand family pew may also be seen. In the churchyard is a sad epitaph to Samuel Kidwell, aged 11 months, that reads:

> He tasted of life's bitter cup,
> Refused to drink the potions up;
> But turned his little head aside,
> Disgusted with the taste – and died.

Behind two thatched cottages are the twin towers of the Elizabethan gatehouse of *Tawstock Court*, burnt down in 1787 and rebuilt in the 'Gothick' style (now a school).

Teigngrace   3C
Village off A382, 3m NW of Newton Abbot

Now barely signposted, Teigngrace was once an important place associated with the transport of granite from Dartmoor to Newton Abbot via the Haytor railway system of 1820. Nearby is the handsome *Stover House* of 1776 (enlarged 1820), now a prestigious girls' school. The *Church of St Peter and St Paul* (1786) is worth a visit on account of its lavish monuments to the Templer family (who built Stover House), including one showing a wreck with men clinging to a rock. Between 1786-1806 three Templers drowned at sea.

Teignmouth   3C
Pop 13,200. 8m N of Torquay (A379). EC Thur.
Inf: Tel (06267) 6271 ext 207

Built on a steep hill, Teignmouth has a lot of unspoiled charm and many unexpected vistas, with its busy harbour tucked away so that a visitor may not even come across it. The town has a bloody history, from Danish and French raiders (the latter burnt the town twice, in 1340 and again in 1690). Most recently the town was heavily bombed in the last war. In the Middle Ages Teignmouth was an important port, and its recent revitalisation dates from the trade in china clay, quarried inland near Newton Abbot. The town was described as a fashionable watering place as early as 1803, but the overall appearance is decidely Victorian and spacious, partly due to *The Den*, 6 acres of well-planted gardens running parallel with the front. There are all the amenities of a family seaside resort: a promenade and pier, a splendid lido, a miniature railway, a bowling green, putting greens and tennis courts. There is a well-kept *Aquarium* and above the town is a first-class golf course. The *Museum* in French Street records the town's history and growth.

Teignmouth has had its share of celebrities; the poet John Keats stayed here, and Jane Austen visited the town in 1801, forming a romantic attachment with a young clergyman who unfortunately died. Across the estuary of the Teign and reached by bridge or passenger ferry is *Shaldon*, and the river itself teems with bird life.

Throwleigh   3B
Dartmoor village off A382, 11m NW of
Moretonhampstead

One of a ring of tiny villages in large parishes that circle Dartmoor. Most of the parish consists of open moor (grazing animals) but around the village are lush farms and woods. The village consists of little more than a handful of beautiful thatched cottages grouped below the 15th-c. church, and the whole composition is one of the most peaceful to be found in England. Villagers and visitors in need of refreshment have to walk 1m S of the village to the admirable *Northmere Arms* – a traditional farmers' pub. Nearby is the parish of *Gidleigh.

Thurlestone 4B
Village on S coast, 5m W of Kingsbridge

A charming seaside village close to Bigbury Bay with one of the best and safest beaches in the county, and renowned for its golf course and riding facilities. The name means 'pierced rock' and this can be seen, a natural arch. The village boasts a fine 16th-c. *Church House* in the main street, as well as the delightful thatched cottages with their flower-filled gardens.

Tiverton 2C/2D
Pop 16,190. 15m N of Exeter (A396). Event: Fair (1st Thur in Jun & Oct) EC Thur MD Tue & Sat. Inf: Tel (0884) 256295

In the Middle Ages Tiverton (two-ford-town) was dominated by the feudal Earls of Devon. From the 13th c. it prospered as a wool town, and textiles remain important today. Despite a disastrous fire in 1731, a number of old buildings of great interest remain.

Tiverton Castle, once home of the Courtenay family, Earls of Devon, commands the N approach to the town. Built by command of Henry I, and being of great strategic importance, it was dismantled by command of Cromwell in 1645. Much remains, including the SE tower (containing a clock collection), the battlemented gatehouse and a later well-furnished mansion. Next to it stands **St Peter's Church** (11th-c., altered in 15th and 16th c.) set in a lovely churchyard with well-trimmed yews. The exterior is exciting with a Norman doorway on the N side and wild gargoyles and carvings all around (note particularly the Tudor ship carvings in the S porch). Inside, the Greenway Chantry Chapel (1517) has a fine carved ceiling.

From the church turn left into Newport Street, passing *The Old Lamb Inn*, and you come to *Castle Street*, an old street with the medieval leat (before the days of plumbing, an open sewer) flowing down the middle. At the end of Newport Street walk down Bampton Street, passing the *Old Corn Market* (1732) where John Wesley preached, and at the end turn left into Gold Street. Opposite are *Greenway's Almshouses* (1517), with an alley at the side leading into the quadrangle. Continue along Gold Street, passing the *statue of Edward VII* on the bridge (River Lowman), and turn right down Station Road. Behind an imposing stone wall is **Old Blundell's School** (not open), founded in 1604 by a wool merchant. One of John Wesley's brothers was headmaster here. Last century the school moved to less cramped premises on the Taunton Road. Retrace your steps and walk along Fore Street. At the end is *St George's Church*, a mellow building of 1730, and beyond it down St Andrew's Street is **Tiverton Museum**, one of Devon's best museums, with excellent folk collections including a Victorian laundry and village smithy. Walk back up St Peter Street past some fine old buildings to the church.

2m N of the town is *Knightshayes Court* (NT), the home of the Heathcoat-Amory family whose ancestor John Heathcoat founded Tiverton's 19th-c. textile industry. 4m S is *Bickleigh* with its craft and farm centre and castle. The *Grand Western Canal* starts in Tiverton and offers beautiful walking (see *Walk 12*, p.27) and horse-drawn boat trips.

Topsham 3D
Town on River Exe off A376, 4m SE of Exeter

Originally a Roman supply port, and from 1290 Exeter's port, Topsham is rich in 17th and 18th-c. houses. Many of them are Dutch in style, and the tiny *Museum* in the Strand is in the sail loft of one of them. The town has many pubs and *The Salutation Inn* in Fore Street dating from 1726 is well worth a visit. The *Church* was over-ethusiastically restored in 1869-78, but has a Norman font which depicts a wolf with an apple in its mouth. The approach from Exmouth across flat estuary land is very picturesque. There is an interesting walk along the River Exe and canal to Exeter (see *Walk 11*, p.26).

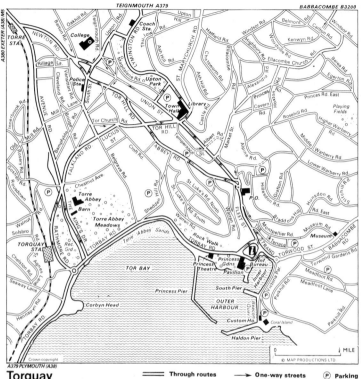

Torquay

Through routes ➡ One-way streets Ⓟ Parking

Torbay 3C/4C
S coast area between St Mary's Bay
and Maidencombe (22m)

This is the most popular tourist region
in Devon, with fine coastal scenery,
unusual for its sub-tropical vegetation
which flourishes in the mild climate.
There are fine beaches and resorts, most
notably the three major centres of
★Torquay, ★Paignton and ★Brixham, and
the lovely village of ★Cockington. See
also ★Berry Head, the promontory at the
S end of the bay.

Torbay Aircraft Museum 4C
Museum at Blagdon, 1m N of A385, 3m W of
Paignton

A fascinating collection of 20 aircraft,
with photographs, documents and Nazi
relics illustrating the history of aviation,
especially during World War II.

Torbay and Dartmouth Railway
See *Dart Valley Railway*

Torcross 4C
Village on S coast (A379), 7m E of Kingsbridge

In 1859, Torcross was 'much frequented by the neighbouring gentry as a
watering place'. It is little changed and
is still popular with visitors who enjoy
the good fishing and walking nearby.
During World War II the area was
evacuated and used by the US Army for
rehearsing the D Day landings (1944).
An obelisk nearby commemorates the
villagers' co-operation. Torcross is most
familiar for the battering it received a
few years ago in ferocious gales. ★*Slapton
Ley* lakeside path runs near the village, a
1½m walk within the celebrated wildlife sanctuary.

Torquay 3C/4C
Pop 56,900. 22m S of Exeter (A380). EC Wed.
Inf: Tel (0803) 27428

Built on seven hills in a sheltered position, Torquay is the chief town of the English Riviera and one of England's major resorts. Prior to the coming of the railways (1840s) and the rapid rise in popularity of holidays at the seaside, Torquay had a population of less than 2000. Today it has thousands of hotels, guest houses and holiday flats.

About 100,000 years ago the earliest settlers in the area occupied **Kent's Cavern** (off the Babbacombe Road, 1m from the harbour) where prehistoric remains of men, hyenas, mammoths, sabre-toothed tigers and cave bears have been found. It is one of the oldest dwellings in the country, and with its weirdly shaped stalagmites is very interesting to visit. In the *Torquay Museum* (Babbacombe Road, ¼m from the harbour) many of the remains excavated from the cavern can be seen.

The other important old site is **Torre Abbey** (off The Front, S of harbour). A Cistercian abbey was founded here in 1196. The gatehouse of 1320 remains intact, but the rest of the buildings were destroyed after the Dissolution in 1539, and are now in ruins. However, the land was acquired in 1662 by the Carey family, who subsequently built a house on the site of the monastic refectory, guest hall and abbot's lodging. The ground floor rooms contain fine furniture and silver, while the 1st and 2nd floors are used as an art gallery. In the grounds is the *Spanish Barn*, actually the abbey tithe barn built in 1196, but so called because 397 Spanish prisoners captured from the Armada were incarcerated in it in 1588.

The other delights of Torquay are those of a major seaside resort: theatres, good beaches, swimming pools, roller-skating, amusement arcades, golf (a very good course), putting and *Aqualand* (on the sea-front), the largest aquarium in the SW. The SW's only Five Star Hotel is in Torquay, the

famed *Imperial Hotel*, and at *Babbacombe* is a very popular *Model Village* (which actually includes a town and farms), illuminated at night with miniature streetlamps. There is also a rack-and-pinion railway here, running down the cliffs to the sea.

Near Torquay is the lovely *Cockington Village*, *Torbay Aircraft Museum*, and *Paignton* with its zoo.

Torrington
See *Great Torrington*

Totnes 4C
Town on A381, 9m S of Newton Abbot.
Event: Elizabethan Day (every Tue, Jun-Sep).
EC Thur MD Fri. Inf: Tel (0803) 863168

A Saxon town, with a Norman castle, Totnes is one of the most unspoilt towns in the SW and has a great deal to interest the visitor. From the Totnes the River Dart is tidal, and from the *bridge* (1826) at the bottom of Fore Street can be seen the timber warehouses and surprisingly large ships that are used for importing wood – Totnes's major industry.

The island in the Dart (reached from the bridge) is a pleasant place to sit, and *The Plains*, the road that runs parallel to the river, is famous for the home (at No 3) of William Wills, the explorer of Australia; but the major attractions of the town are **Fore Street** and **High Street**, full of medieval and Tudor buildings (mostly refaced in the 18th and 19th c.).

Walking up Fore Street, the first important building is the **Elizabethan House** on the left, now a delightful and well-displayed museum of items of local interest, including old ivory false teeth! The restored *East Gate* over the street is on the site of one of Totnes's three medieval gates. The Rampart Walk, to the right, follows the line of the old city wall to the **Guildhall**, on the site of 13th-c. monastic buildings. Enlarged in the 16th c., the panelled council chamber and mayor's parlour are still in regular use. The beautiful magistrate's court was last used in 1974, and it is longer still since the old lock-up was used. Opposite is **St Mary's Church**, a spacious 15th-c. red sandstone building with a delicate filigree screen (1460) and superb pulpit, pew fronts and ceilings. Emerging through the S porch you return to the High Street. Just down the hill at No 10A is the *Devonshire Collection of Period Costume*.

Up the hill are the covered *Poultry Walk* and *Butter Walk*. Up to Victorian times markets were held in the open, but butter always had to be sold in the shade to prevent it from melting, hence the Butter Walk. At the top of the town, but with its entrance from a side-street off to the right, is **Totnes Castle**, a classic Norman motte and bailey. Built to defend the crossing over the River Dart, the castle has commanding views over the town and surrounding hills. Near the entrance to the castle is the arch of the town's former *North Gate*.

Totnes Motor Museum in Bridgetown, just the other side of the River Dart, has a collection of working vintage and veteran cars. Adjacent to it is *The Steam Packet Inn*, from where a cruiser can be taken down the beautiful Dart valley to *Dartmouth*. 2m NE is the *Dartington Hall* complex of arts centre and craftshops, and 3m NE are the haunted ruins of *Berry Pomeroy Castle*.

Summer Tuesdays in Totnes are *Elizabethan Day*, when a number of locals dress up in period costume.

Trentishoe 1B

Village on N coast off A39, 10m W of Lynton

This tiny hamlet with little more than two farmsteads is a good centre for exploring one of the most exciting stretches of the N Devon coastline. The minute **St Peter's Church** nestles by a farmhouse ½m from the sea in a sheltered vale. Although so small, the church has a musicians' gallery (1771), which in turn is so small that a hole was cut in the parapet to accommodate the local farmer's double-bass.

Nearby is *Heddon's Mouth*, a renowned rocky valley in the care of the National Trust, and there is superb woodland and cliff scenery all around, with views across the Bristol Channel to Wales.

Two Bridges 3B

Dartmoor village on B3212 nr Princetown, 18m NE of Plymouth

This tiny hamlet on Dartmoor, named after the two bridges (of 1780 and 1928) over the West Dart River, was once an important road junction. It is a good base for walking, and many visitors have thanked their stars for its existence when they have been on foot and, always dangerous on Dartmoor, lost. There is a pleasant inn. See also *Wistman's Wood*.

Uffculme 2D

Village on B3391, 5m NE of Cullompton

An attractive 18th-c. village with many fine houses. Of particular note are *Ayshford House* (1701) W of the square, and *Bengal House*. In the High Street is a factory (1838) with an octagonal tower. *St Mary's Church* (15th-c.) is important for the Walrond Chapel, with its unusual family tomb, and the exceptional 67ft-wide screen. The wooden *Shambles* or market area in the square dates from the 14th c.

By the river S of the village is **Coldharbour Mill**, in use from the late 18th c. until 1981 for the manufacture of woven cloth. It has now been coverted into a working museum of the woollen and worsted industry by the Coldharbour Mill Trust. The old watermill and steam engine are still operating and visitors can see cloth produced as in Victorian times. Woollen articles can be purchased from the shop, and the mill grounds, set in the attractive Culm Valley, are perfect for a picnic.

Ugborough 4B

Village off B3210, 12m E of Plymouth

That Devonians were pagans long before they were Christians is well illustrated in Ugborough, where the church and churchyard are built within a small prehistoric camp. The *Church* is 15th-c., and there are traces of 16th-c. paintings on the imposing screen and an interesting brass to an unknown lady. N of the village and over the A38 is *Ugborough Beacon* (1231ft).

Ugbrooke House 3C
Historic house off A380 nr Chudleigh, 6m N of Newton Abbot

A castellated mansion *c.* 1760 with battlements and towers, designed by Robert Adam. The magnificent gardens and lakes were laid out by Capability Brown. It is lived in and run by the ancient Clifford family, and during the summer season a programme of events is arranged for most Sundays, including Rolls-Royce rallies, horse-shows, model aircraft flights, etc. The house contains a wealth of objects associated with the Clifford family, including some fine pictures, magnificent tapestries and an embroidery collection. In the park are lakes, a large aviary and many colourful rhododendrons.

Valley of the Rocks
See *Lynton and Lynmouth*

Watermouth Castle 1B (nr Berrynarbor)
Leisure centre on A399, 2m E of Ilfracombe

Really a castellated mansion of 1825, Watermouth has been taken over as an entertainments centre. The Great Hall and a number of the rooms contain varied attractions and curiosities: a model railway, antique self-playing musical instruments, pier machines etc. There are also crafts, a pet's corner and aviary.

Watersmeet
See *Lynton and Lynmouth*

Wembury 4B
Village on S coast off A379, 8m SE of Plymouth

Offshore is the *Great Mew Stone*, an impressive triangular rock. Boldly sited on a cliff overlooking the sea is the *Church of St Werburgh*, a landmark since the 14th c. The church contains some interesting monuments, notably the colossal one to Sir John Hele (d1608) 'covered in busty ladies'. Nearby are several large houses such as *Langdon Court*, an Elizabethan mansion of 1577, now a convalescent home, and *Wembury House* of 1803. There is a well-established coastal walk along the *South West Coast Path* from Wembury

to Stoke House, a distance of 7m, with an agreeable interlude by ferry over the river Yealm (summer only). The varied walks go through woodland as well as along cliffs (mostly National Trust), and there are many secluded coves reached only by fellow walkers.

Westward Ho! 1A
Village on N coast (B3236), 3m NW of Bideford

It is not often that a village is built to commemorate a book, but Westward Ho! enjoys this distinction. Named after the historical novel by Charles Kingsley, the village began in 1863 when the Duchess of Portland laid the foundation stone. The literary association goes further: Rudyard Kipling was one of the first pupils in the village and based *Stalky and Co* on his experiences here. He is honoured with a magnificent stretch of cliffs on the W of the village named after him. A guide book of 1872 says: 'Westward Ho! consists at present of two or three rows of terraces, many scattered villas, a single line of shops and a church nearly opposite the principal hotel.' Things have changed since then, and to many the best part of this amiable, if less than beautiful seaside resort is the 2m-long *Pebble Ridge* and superb sandy beach. Good golf course and first-class surfing.

Widecombe-in-the-Moor 3C
Dartmoor village off A38, 9m N of Ashburton
Event: Widecombe Fair. (early Sep.)

Set in one of the lushest parts of Dartmoor, Widecombe-in-the-Moor can be seen for miles on account of its granite church tower (130ft high). The 14th-c. **St Pancras' Church** is known as the 'cathedral of the moor' and has a medieval rood screen with 32 painted figures on it. In 1638 a great storm with vivid flashes of lighting struck the church, killing 4 and injuring 62. It was said to be the work of the Devil, who was seen riding through the village dressed in black on a black charger. The dark figure was known to be Satan because when he had stopped at an inn in the village, the beer sizzled as he poured it down his throat.

In the village square *Church House*, owned by the National Trust, is an impressive 15th-c. building now used as a hall and cottage. Opposite, also built from local stone, is the grand *Glebe House*. Widecombe is celebrated for its annual fair (held in early September) made famous by Uncle Tom Cobley, who is remembered by a stone plaque on the village green.

A few minutes' walk from the village centre down Venton Lane is *Little Meadow Cottage Industry*. Well worth a visit, wicker-work and hand carving in wood and stone are carried out on the premises. 2m NW of the village are *Hameldown Beacon* (1697ft) and *Hameldown Tor* (1736ft), the highest peaks in West Dartmoor, and the Bronze Age enclosure of *Grimspound*.

Wistman's Wood 3B
Natural feature on footpath 2m N of intersection of B3357 & B3212, 22m NE of Plymouth

The wood can be approached from *Postbridge* to the N or *Two Bridges* to the S, the latter being slightly nearer, but both routes involve a strenuous walk of up to 1 hr. The wood, which is only 700 yds long and half as wide, is described in a guide-book of 1859 as 'so weird in appearance, so stunted and misshapen in its growth, so impenetrable from the nature of the ground, and exhibiting such singular marks of age, that it cannot fail to excite the most lively wonder and astonishment'. It is the last remaining part of the primeval forest that once covered all of Dartmoor and is traditionally a sacred site for the Druids.

Woodbury 3D
Village on B3179, 8m SE of Exeter

Beautifully situated amidst lush woodland, Woodbury serves as an excellent centre for walking and contains the charming and characterful *Plumbers' Arms* pub. The *Church* dates from 1409 and has a notable Elizabethan altar as well as other good woodwork. Nearby, overlooking the Exe estuary, is *Woodbury Castle*, an Iron Age encampment, spreading over 5 acres. The site was subsequently used by the Romans (a Roman road passes by the camp) and again for defences against a Napoleonic invasion.

Woolacoombe 1A
Village on N coast (B3343) 6m SW of Ilfracombe. Inf: Tel (0271) 870553

The 2m of magnificent golden sandy beaches, with excellent surfing, are probably the best in Britain. *Barricane Beach* is a mecca for shell-collectors, and Woolacombe Downs support a wide variety of plant life. On a clear day, 20 miles to the W, can be seen *Lundy Island*.

Yealmpton 4B
Village on A379, 7m SE of Plymouth

A pleasant place noteworthy for the *Devon Shire Farm Centre* (1m SE of the village), a 60-acre farm where all the work is done by Shire horses, with foals, carts and a blacksmith's shop. *St Bartholomew's Church* is Victorian, with local marble used inside. There is a monumental brass (1508) from a previous church on the site, and also a monument to the local squires, a family with the unfortunate name of Bastard. A very quaint building (now a restaurant) is *Mother Hubbard's Cottage*, with its lopsided thatched roof and windows set at odd angles. This actually *is* the home of Mother Hubbard, created by Mrs Sarah Martin who lived at Kitley, the home of the Bastards. 1m SW by the river are *Kitley Caves*, discovered by quarrymen in 1800, where prehistoric bones of bears, hyenas and woolly elephants, have been found.

Yelverton 3B
Dartmoor village on A386, 10m N of Plymouth

A village in the shadow of Sheepstor with a church, built on a plateau, notable for its view rather than architecture (1914). The interest lies in the *Paperweight Centre*, a collection of over 800 with a wide range for sale. It advertises itself as 'Devon's indoor beauty spot'.

Index

95